EQUITY

VALUATION

:: Author ::

Prakash Parmar
(M.Com., B.ed.,NET., M.B.A)

PUBLISHED BY

The New Era International Publishing House
HQ. At & Po. Chaveli., Ta- Chansma,
Dist- Patan, North Gujarat, India, Asia.
www.iphouseindia.com

First Publication: 23rd March, 2015

Copyright: Author

(c) **Prakash Parmar**

ISBN:- 978-15-08949-89-3

Price: Rs.800/- INDIA

$ 15 OUTSIDE INDIA

PUBLISHED BY

The New Era International Publishing House
HQ. At & Po. Chaveli., Ta- Chansma,
Dist- Patan, North Gujarat, India, Asia.
www.iphouseindia.com

Equity Valuation: Definition, Importance and Process

Throughout finance, one rule always holds true. The general belief is that the value of any asset or security is exactly equal to the discounted present value of all the cash flows that can be derived from it in future periods.

Using this principle, one can easily value securities like debt. This is because they have a finite existence. The cash flows derived from them can be easily predicted. However, equity valuation is not so simple. Equity represents a partnership in the business. As such, it represents an attempt to value cash flows which are uncertain and unpredictable.

In this , we will try to understand the concept of equity valuation in more detail.

Definition

In finance, valuation is a process of determining the fair market value of an asset. Equity valuation therefore refers to the process of determining the fair market value of equity securities.

Importance of Equity Valuation: Systemic

The whole system of stock markets is based upon the idea of equity valuation. The stock markets have a wide variety of stocks on offer, whose perceived market value changed every minute because of the change in information that the market receives on a real time basis.

Equity valuation therefore is the backbone of the modern financial system. It enables companies with sound business models to command a premium in the market. On the other hand, it ensures that companies whose fundamentals are weak witness a drop in their valuation. The art and science of equity valuation therefore enables the modern economic system to efficiently allocate scare capital resources amongst various market participants.

Importance of Equity Valuation: Individual

As discussed, on a micro level, equity valuation is beneficial for the entire stock market ecosystem. However, how does it benefit an individual to study and apply the principles of equity valuation?

Well, markets receive information every moment and make an attempt to factor the financial effect of this information in the stock price. Individual estimates of the effect vary and as such different people may come up with different stock prices. Therefore, there can be a difference between the market value of a company and what investors call its true or "intrinsic value"

Investors, stand to gain a lot of money if they are able to correctly identify this difference. The second richest person in the world, Warren Buffett has made his fortune correcting and applying the art of equity valuation. In fact, the theory of equity valuation has been heavily influenced by the work of Warren Buffett and his mentor.

Process of Conducting Equity Valuation

Equity valuation is followed differently by different individuals. As such, there is no set pre-defined standard process. Instead, equity valuation consists of 4 or 5 broad categories of steps that need to be followed. The procedures maybe different but the objectives are always the same. Every person conducting equity valuation, must in one way or another account for these parameters:

1. **Understand the macroeconomic factors and the industry:** No company operates in vacuum. As such, the performance of every business is influenced by the performance of the economy in general as well as the industry in which it operates. As such, before making an attempt to value a business, the macro-economic factors must be accounted for. A reasonably accurate prediction regarding these parameters creates the base for an accurate valuation.

2. **Make a reasonable forecast of the company's performance:** Mere extrapolation of the company's current financial statements does not constitute a good forecast. A good forecast takes into account how the company may change its scale of production of the forthcoming future. Then, it also takes into account how changes in this scale will affect the costs. Costs and sales do not move in linear fashion. To come up with an accurate forecast, an analyst would require intricate knowledge of the company's business.

3. **Select the appropriate valuation model:** Valuation is less of a science and more of an art. There are multiple valuation models available. Also, all these valuation models do not necessarily lead to the same conclusion. Hence, it is the job of the analyst to understand which model would be most appropriate given the type and quality of data available.

4. **Arrive at a valuation figure based on the forecast:** The next step is to apply the valuation model and come up with an exact numerical value which according to the analyst defines the worth of the business. It may be a single estimated amount or it could be a range. Investors prefer a range so that they clearly know what their lower and upper bounds for bidding should be.

5. **Take action based on the arrived valuation:** Finally, the analyst has to give a buy, sell or hold recommendation based on the current market price and what analysis shows is the intrinsic worth of the company.

The process of equity valuation is thus long, subjective and difficult to understand. However, for those who do master this art, the rewards are enormous.

Market Value, Intrinsic Value and Investment Value

Equity valuation or the valuation of any asset is an art. Valuation is not a perfect science and there is no single correct answer to what the value of a security ought to be. Valuation is at best, an informed guess or an informed opinion. As such, when analysts use the term value, they might be using it to describe one of the many concepts that can fall under the umbrella term called "value". As students, we must therefore be aware of the different types of concepts related to valuation. This will explain in detail, the three most popular ones:

Market Value

Market value is the easiest valuation concept to understand. It simply means the value of the company or an asset as denoted by its ongoing market price. As market prices vary wildly, so does the market value of any company or any asset which is listed on it.

Students tend to get confused trying to find out the difference between market valuation and market price. The truth is that there is no difference at all! The fundamental idea is that markets are efficient and at any point of time the prices reflected by the markets are an informed decision made by the market. The market price therefore is the same thing as market valuation and is based on the idea of efficient market hypothesis.

Intrinsic Value

The concept of intrinsic value has been made famous by famous investors from value investing school like Warren Buffet, Benjamin Graham etc. In simple words, intrinsic value is that value which is imbibed in the asset. For instance, a machine may provide certain incremental benefits to its user over and above what manual labor could have. As such the machine provides incremental cash flows to the firm and has some amount of intrinsic value.

The value of a firm is nothing but the sum total of the value that will be provided by its assets over some selected time horizon. As such, just like the intrinsic value of an asset can be estimated, similarly the intrinsic value of an entire firm can also be estimated.

It is important to understand that the intrinsic value can only be accurately understood and calculated by someone who has an in-depth knowledge of the nature of the firm and the industry. Intrinsic value, calculated by analysts who are armchair experts is often way off the mark and grossly miscalculates what the correct value of the firm should be. Hence, while considering intrinsic value, one must compare and contrast the opinions of multiple analysts.

Investment Value

Intrinsic value looks at the value of a firm in isolation. It only considers that value which can be derived from incremental cash flows that will be produced by a firm. However, consider the case of an oligarch who faces only one competitor. This competitor is driving down the prices that the oligarch could otherwise charge from the customers. Hence, in such a case, if the oligarch can buy out the competitor, he will be able to eliminate the competition and become a monopolist. The benefits that will arise obviously cannot be computed using a simple discounted cash flow application. This may not be an ethical scenario. However, business has in the past witnessed these situations and in all likelihood will witness them in the future as well.

The point being made here is that sometimes corporations experience synergy when they combine their business. Hence, some competitors may be able and willing to pay more for an asset or a company if its fits well with their existing business. This valuation is called investment value. The recent acquisition of Whatsapp by Facebook is one such example of the use of investment value in real life scenarios.

It needs to be understood that investment value is subjective for each buyer. The synergies depend upon the current portfolio of assets that are owned by the acquirer and their strategic vision. Hence, Facebook, Yahoo, Google could have all pitched in for the acquisition of Whatsapp. However, the valuation that they arrive upon will depend upon the strategic fit of Whatsapp in their future plans. Since each company will have a different mix of assets and a different vision for the future. Hence, each company will arrive at a different valuation.

Once again, investment value is subjective. It does not depend upon the asset. Rather, it depends upon the buyer.

Hence, when the term value or value creation is used, it is possible that any one of these concepts is being referred to. An analyst or even a student for that matter must have a clear understanding regarding which measure of value is applicable in which context.

Applications of Equity Valuation

"Valuation" or the process of assigning a fixed numerical value to the present and potential of a business is considered by many experts to be the most important part of corporate finance and financial markets. The most coveted and highly paid jobs in the financial markets are in this domain.

The reason for this is that the accuracy of the value derived can never be known. It is not a verifiable fact and there is no right or wrong answer. Rather, the valuation is an opinion that is based on the expertise of the person conducting the exercise.

Now, if we take the subjectivity and add to it the fact that decisions involving billions of dollars have to be taken based on the valuation, we see why it is arguably the most important task in finance. Let's see the kind of decisions that need to be made based on the value derived from equity valuation.

Stock Picking

The most common application of equity valuation is related to stock picking. In a world with perfect markets, stock picking would be a futile exercise. All the stocks would always be valued correctly and it would be impossible to make any supernormal profits from investing in these stocks. However, fortunately or unfortunately, we do not live in this world with perfect markets.

The theory of stock selection is based on the flaws of the market. The belief is that in the short run, due to investor euphoria or pessimism, stocks tend to be valued on the market at more or less price than what they are actually worth. Thus, if one has an objective basis to find out the true intrinsic value of these stocks, one can gain while buying in a depressed market and selling later when markets return to normal.

Therefore, it is implied that any investor must always have their own estimate of value of the stock, which they derive from their very own equity valuation model. Then they must constantly be on the lookout for undervalued stocks or as Warren Buffet puts it, "dollar bills which are selling for ten cents in the market."

Estimating the Market Sentiment

This is a slightly unconventional application of the field of equity valuation. Now, there are times when the market can be seen to be clearly euphoric and there are other times when the market seems to be clearly depressed. However, sometimes the signals may not be so clear and investors may be clueless as to what the market's expectations of the future are.

In this case too, equity valuation can come to the rescue. The idea is to arrive at a fair valuation and then compare them with the values prevalent in the market. If the market is overvaluing most of the stocks, then investors are expecting a positive future and the sentiment is positive. The converse of this is also true. Hence, equity valuation can be used as a tool to read the market.

Listing Of Private Businesses

Private businesses and capital markets have a symbiotic relationship. Private businesses can obtain cheap funds from the capital markets, whereas investors get a chance to invest in lucrative businesses by being in the capital markets.

However, when a private business initially lists itself on the market and becomes a public company, it faces a problem. How do the owners and investors know what the correct value of the business is? What is the right price for the investors to pay and for the owners to accept? Well, once again the art and science of valuation comes to the rescue. Using equity valuation models, analysts can arrive at a relatively precise price supported by facts and data which is usually acceptable to both the counterparties involved in the trade.

Valuing the business is therefore the number one task that needs to be performed by merchant bankers when they plan on taking a company public.

Mergers and Acquisitions

Lastly, just like listing of private businesses, there is also considerable ambiguity over the price to be paid when mergers and acquisitions happen. How do the investors of both companies know that they are getting a fair deal? Well, once again, equity valuation comes to the rescue. The valuation exercise here is quite complicated. First both individual entities need to be valued and then the combined entity needs to be valued. Then gains from merging the business or "synergy" have to be found out.

Later, based on the bargaining power and the risk-reward bearing agreement of the venture, a fair valuation can be arrived at which is acceptable to both the acquirer and the acquired.

To sum it up, valuation is the lifeblood of financial services. All sorts of organizations, from merchant banks to portfolio management companies need this knowledge. Also, it is an imperfect knowledge hence companies are willing to spend more and more money to hire people they believe have a good understanding of the concept of valuation.

Assumptions Used In Equity Valuation

Equity valuation is about guessing what the value of an organization is expected to be a decade from now or an even bigger time horizon. Obviously, the financial future, just like future in general is difficult to predict.

However, in equity valuation, one cannot proceed further until some assumptions are made about the future. Every analyst report that we read is therefore making some assumptions about the future. Some of these assumptions will be explicitly stated whereas others will be implied in the report.

The important thing to realize is that any report or stock valuation is only as good as the assumptions that it is built upon. If we, as investors, do not agree with the assumptions on which the report is based, we do not agree with the report in general!

A good investor, therefore consciously scans equity valuation reports for assumptions that have been made, validates them and only then proceeds to critically evaluate the report. If any discrepancies are found, investors may adjust the assumptions to arrive at what they feel is the fair value of the investment.

Let's look at some of the common assumptions that are made during the investment process:

Going Concern Assumption:

The first and the most basic assumption that is made by analysts is the going concern assumption. It does not matter which model is being used or whether it is the cash flows that are being discounted or the dividends are, the analyst and therefore the investor are assuming that the company will continue to be in business for the foreseeable future.

This assumption is usually valid as most companies do in fact stay in business over a period of time. However, if investors are taking a bearish stand on a stock and expect the company to shut down in the near future, they must ensure that they value the company based on the liquidation assumption and not on the going concern assumption which is usually the case.

Re-investment Assumptions:

To forecast, future cash flows which may be 5 or 10 years down the line, analysts have to make assumptions about how the proceeds that the company will generate over the same period will be used. Or if they believe that the company is growing at a rate which is faster than that which can be financed by internal accruals, they also have to make assumptions regarding from where and at what cost will that money be arranged by the company. These assumptions must be grounded in reality i.e. the assumption of more investment must be supported by a bigger market which the company is trying to enter and the availability of human and other resources to do so!

This is one of the most fundamental assumptions in equity valuation. Different analysts have different visions for how the company plans to conduct its business in the future. These different assumptions are the root cause behind different valuations.

Many times analysts connect with the senior management of the company, specifically to know their long term plans so that they can plan the cash flows accordingly. These assumptions will usually be stated in the report itself.

Dividend Payout Assumptions:

Based on the past dividend payout of the company, its expected growth rates and its free cash flow, investors can make an educated guess of what the dividend payout ratio for any given company will be. These dividend payments are cash flows which go out of the firm and therefore slow down the growth rate. It is important to understand the validity of the dividend payout assumption as the valuation of the company can be significantly changed even if minor adjustments are made in dividend payouts.

Macro-Economic Assumptions:

All the assumptions that are to be made are not company specific. The company is a part of the macro economy in general. Therefore, any changes in the macro economy are also expected to affect the company. Analysts therefore use forecasts by bodies like IMP, World Bank etc as their assumptions. Since these forecasts come from bodies which are experts in their field, they are the best estimate that an analyst can really make. However, even these bodies have a dismal record when it comes to predicting the future state of the economy. Hence, it is exceedingly difficult to get accurate data about the economy even though it forms one of the most fundamental assumptions.

Industry Assumptions:

Lastly, analysts also make assumptions about how the different competitors of the company will fare. This is done as a part of industry analysis. No company operates in vacuum and hence the performance of any given company can be seen as linked to that of its peers. Assumptions regarding change in market share or market leadership must be based on sound data and foreseeable competitive advantages. Analysts have a difficult time predicting changed in the industry as well.

However, this is easier to do as compared to macro economic analysis.

Thus, every equity valuation report has explicit and implicit assumptions. The job of an investor is to carefully study the validity of these assumptions before they believe in the contents of the report and make decisions accordingly!

Qualitative Issues While Conducting Equity Valuation

Equity valuation focuses on estimating what the likelihood of the company being a successful enterprise in the future is. Now, it is difficult to construct any model which can predict the success of any enterprise. For example, consider the fact that new age companies like Google and Facebook share almost none of the characteristics that were present in behemoths like Exxon, Wal-Mart or even Apple for that matter.

There are however, some questions that need to be addressed before a valuation exercise is undertaken. These issues are not quantitative and do not find direct application in the valuation report. These questions, however are qualitative and hence indirectly influence the valuation exercise. Here are some of the important qualitative issues:

Industry Analysis: Industry analysis is of prime importance. Companies always compete with each other to obtain a share of the same market. Hence, if a company's competitors become more powerful and efficient then it stands to lose out. In the modern market, no innovation does not mean stagnation rather it means the end of the enterprise as more efficient competitors will sooner or later put you out of business.

Hence, equity analysts try to dig through industry journals and have a keen eye on which company is conducting what research. They also use the Porter's five forces model to gauge whether or not, the industry as a whole is losing its attractiveness to another industry.

Strategy: The next qualitative question to be addressed is the company's strategic vision. Usually, all companies will follow one of the three strategies. They will either try to be:

1. Cost leaders i.e. provide the product or service at the lowest price to the consumers. An example of this would be Wal-Mart

2. Innovators i.e. providers of superior quality products and constantly developing new and better products. An example of this would be Apple

3. Niche service providers i.e. providers of products and services for a very specific group of customers, whose needs are well understood by them i.e. Harley Davidson motorcycles

Each of these strategies requires a very different approach. For instance, cost leadership requires supply chain superiority, innovation requires focus on research and development and niche services requires focus on customer relationship management. Analysts need to be aware of the strategy of the company, their investments towards building the capabilities required to service this strategy and also the developments that the competitors are making in this regard.

Quality of Financial Statements:

The last, but the most important issue in equity valuation is the quality of financial statements supplied by the companies. Now, we may all like to believe that accounting is a standardized process and there is only one way to account for transactions. However, that is not true. Accounting can be highly subjective. Many times companies provide financial statements which do comply with the reporting norms. However, they are opaque and do not really provide the required information.

Quality of earnings has been a burning issue in equity valuation especially after scams like Enron and WorldCom revealed that the real valuation of these companies was not even a fraction of what was being quoted in the marketplace. Here are some of the tell tale signs that an analyst needs to look for:

1. Premature recognition of income or income smoothening. Many companies attempt to book revenues before they arise. Doing so makes them look more efficient and profitable than they actually are.

2. On the other hand, companies try to delay the recognition of expenses. This is just the converse of premature income recognition.However, it is equally effective in creating the illusion of a successful company.

3. The company's treatment of non operating gains and losses also provides a good idea about the quality of earnings that are being presented by the company.

4. Companies can also make themselves appear more profitable by changing their policies pertaining to depreciation, amortization and capitalization. Changes in these policies must be probed for their effect on the financial statement and the possibility of financial fraud must not be ruled out

5. Also, a lot of companies engage in off balance sheet financing and investing transactions. As per reporting norms, they need not be reported on the balance sheet. However, they do have a material effect on the finances of the firm and hence transactions involving derivatives and special purpose entities (SPE's) must be carefully scrutinized before coming up with a verdict regarding the value of the company.

To sum it up, qualitative factors are also of prime importance in the equity valuation exercise. If it was only about number crunching, then there would have been algorithms developed to do so and the need for humans would be eliminated. However, which numbers should be processed is the big question. This big question can only be answered with the help of an expert!

Intrinsic Value and Mispricing

The whole objective of equity valuation is to find mispriced securities. Investors can make abnormal profits when they find securities which are lower than their intrinsic worth trading in the market. However, the concept of mispricing and intrinsic value is misunderstood to say the least. What the average person considers as mispricing is at best a narrower concept, an estimation of what mispricing truly is. In this , we will explore in detail the concept of mispricing.

Two Layers vs. Three Layers

The average person considered mispricing to be a two layered concept. This means that they believe that there is a given market price and then there is the intrinsic worth of the security i.e. the two layers. They believe that the true intrinsic worth of the security can be calculated with precision and mispriced securities can be discovered.

However, this is not the truth. Since the whole subject of valuation is an imperfect science, the true intrinsic worth of a security can never be found out for sure. At best, we can get approximations. Human error will always be present. A better analyst may provide a more accurate estimate of the intrinsic worth of the security. However, it will still be an estimate and not the intrinsic worth itself.

Hence, finding mispriced securities is about understanding the three layers i.e. the quoted market price, the estimate of intrinsic value and the intrinsic value itself. Hence, there will actually be two gaps which need to be taken into consideration before making an investment decision.

The Two Gaps:

Since there are three layers present and the difference between any two layers forms a gap, there will be two gaps present. The details regarding these gaps are as follows:

- **Gap #1: Market Mispricing:** This is the mispricing that arises because of temporary euphoria and pessimism in the marketplace. Investors start believing that the present boom or doom is permanent and stocks either rise or fall to unrealistic levels. Since this a gap between the quoted market price and the analyst's estimate of intrinsic value, it is called market mispricing. This is a known risk and hence can be controlled. It is driven by the sentiment in the market.

- **Gap # 2: Analyst Mispricing:** On the other hand, analyst mispricing represents the risk that the analyst's estimate of intrinsic value may itself vary significantly from actual intrinsic value of the firm. Since the actual intrinsic value is not known, this is an unknown risk. Every analyst makes the best effort to arrive at the correct valuation. However, because there are so many factors involved it is likely that the estimated intrinsic value may be significantly higher or lower than the actual value. This is an unknown risk and hence more difficult to mitigate.

Mitigating the Two Gaps:

Now, since we are aware that there are actually two types of gaps present, we must understand how professional investors mitigate the risks arising from these gaps. The usual mitigation plans are as follows:

- **Multiple Models:** Firstly, an attempt is made to arrive at the best possible estimate of intrinsic value. For this purpose, instead of using a single model, analysts often use multiple models. The valuations derived from these models may vary significantly from one another. However, the difference in valuations leaves clues to what the drivers of higher valuation as per a given model are.

- **Multiple Analysts:** Secondly, to reduce the risk of person driven errors and to make the valuation exercise more process driven, companies often use multiple analysts. Different analysts think differently and provide their version of what the future prospects for the target company are expected to be. These multiple opinions help in reducing the unknown risk. The risk of analyst mispricing is always present but, to some extent, this exercise reduces its effect.

Single Period Dividend Discount Model

To understand the dividend discount model, we need to start from the basics. The simplest way to understand the dividend discount model and its application is to first start with a single period and then later extend it on to more complex cases. Hence, the term single period dividend discount model.

The objective of application of this model is to derive what the fair market price of the stock should be if we know certain other information about that stock. The other information is the expected future price, expected dividend payout in that single period and the investors required rate of return.

Let's understand the application of a single period dividend discount model with the help of an example:

Example:

An investor is wondering what the correct price of a share should be? He knows that his required rate of return is 9%. He also knows that the share will give a Rs.5 dividend in the current period and the expected market value at the end of the period is Rs.200. What would the fair price for such a stock be?

Calculation:

We know that the value of the stock is equal to the present value of all the future cash flows that can be derived from it. In this case we are getting cash flows in two different forms. One form is dividends and the other form is the final sale proceeds.

Let's call the dividends D1 and the final sale proceeds P1. Thus the total cash flow that we will obtain at the end of the period is D1+P1. Now the next task is to calculate the present value of these cash flows i.e. discount them at the expected rate of return for the investor.

Hence, the formula pertaining to single period dividend discount model is:

Present Market Price = $(D1+P1)/(1+r)$
Therefore, in our case, it equals:
$(Rs.5+Rs.200)/1.09 = Rs.188.07$
Thus, the fair market value of this stock should ideally be Rs.188.07

Interpreting the Results:

In case the investor is fairly confident about all of his/her assumptions then the stock will provide them with a value equal to Rs.188.07 in present value terms.

- Hence, if the price is values at Rs.188.07, the investor may or may not buy the stock. Since it just meets the investor's expectations, there are no abnormal profits to be made
- In case, the price is less than Rs.188.07, then the stock is undervalued and the investor should immediately make the purchase. If the investor's assumptions are correct, he/she stands to make a windfall gain from the buying and selling of this stock
- In case, the price is greater than Rs.188.07, then the investor should refrain from making the purchase. The stock is intrinsically worth less than what the investor would pay off for it and the investor would be better off putting that money in another investment.

Difficulty in Implementation:

The single period dividend model can tell you whether a price is overvalued or undervalued if two variables which will become known only in the future i.e. the future price and the future dividend are accurately predicted today!

Also, while theoretically investors are supposed to know their required rate of return, not many investors actually do! So the third variable being used in the formula is also slightly difficult to predict.

Needless to say, this is not a very good idea. Guessing an accurate dividend itself may be difficult. However, guessing an accurate future price is almost impossible! Therefore, it may seem like this model is not very useful and it really isn't if you consider it on its own.

However, this model forms the building block for later models some of which are based on more realistic assumptions and are therefore much more applicable and helpful.

Absolute Valuation Models Vs Relative Valuation Models

Equity valuation can be conducted using two broad types of models. Of course, each type of models has their own subtypes. However, when it comes to broad classification, there are really only two types of approaches possible. One of them is called the absolute valuation approach whereas the other is called the relative valuation approach. In this , we will explain the difference between these two types of approaches.

1. **Absolute Valuation Models:**

The defining characteristic of an absolute valuation model is that in this model the value of the asset is derived only on the basis of characteristics of that asset. There is no consideration regarding the valuation of other comparable assets that are trading in the marketplace. These models are basically known as the "discounted cash flow" of the DCF models. These models are widely used across the industry. There are several subtypes of discounted cash flow models which we will discuss now:

a. **Discounted Dividend Models:** Discounted dividend models assume that the shareholders of the firm are only entitled to its dividends. Thus, these models assume the purchase price of the share as the initial negative cash outflow and then assume that dividends that will be received throughout the life of the firm are the positive cash flows. Based on the dividends that are expected to be received later, it is decided whether an investment is worthwhile given its current market price.

b. **Discounted Free Cash Flow Models:** The discounted free cash flow models differ from the discounted dividend models in the sense that a broader concept of cash flows is being used. These models look at the total cash flow that will accrue to the firm. Then they subtract the amounts that are owed to outside parties like government, bondholders etc. They balance amount is considered free cash flow to the firm. This is projected for several years and then discounted to arrive at the valuation of the firm.

c. **Discounted Residual Income Models:**Discounted residual income models look at an even broader concept of cash flows. They just consider all the cash flows that accrue to the firm post the payment to suppliers and other outside parties. Payments due to bondholders and preference shareholders are also not subtracted from the total. The residual cash flow is then discounted to arrive at the valuation of the firm.

We can see that in all the above models, different variations of the cash flow are being discounted. They are pretty much the same apart from the fact that different cash flows also mean different risk and therefore different discount rates need to be applied to these cash flows to arrive at the appropriate valuation.

d. **Discounted Asset Models:**A slightly different absolute valuation model is the discounted asset model. In this case, the valuation is conducted based upon the market value of the assets that the firm currently owns. The present value of each asset is derived and then all the values of all the assets are added up to come up with a value for the entire corporation. This method does not take into account the synergy between the assets. As such, it can only be used for commodity businesses which involve oil, coal or other such natural resources.

2. **Relative Valuation Models:** Relative valuation models are different from discounted cash flow models. They are different in the sense that they do not value a firm or an asset based on what its intrinsic value is. Rather, these models believe that the market may be wrong about a given stock. However, for an industry in general the market is right.

Hence, the approach followed in relative valuation models is to find a benchmark valuation. Let's say that when we make an index of all the stocks in the technical industry, we get a market price to earnings ratio of 25. This means that the market believes that each stock is worth approximately 25 times what its current earnings are.

Next, we look at a particular stock. Let's say the stock of Yahoo Inc. We see that Yahoo is valued only at 17 times its earnings even though the market is valued at 25 times its earnings. We then study the details of Yahoo's business to find legitimate reasons as to why it should be so undervalued. If the reasons are found, then the stock is trading at fair value. However, if there is no cause for the stock to trade at a lower P/E than the market, then we assume that this is a market anomaly and that Yahoo shares are trading below their fair value, making them a good buy.

There are many variations of relative valuation models as well. Instead of using price earnings ratio, we could use price to sales ratio, price to book value ratio, price to cash flow ratio or any number of ratios.

Each of these models, have a lot of detailed explanation that needs to be given before they can be finally implemented. This explanation will be given in the later. The purpose of this is to provide a broad overview and give a basic introduction.

Choosing a Valuation Model

Now, since we are aware that there are actually multiple models that can be used to value any given company or asset, the next question that arises is which one should we use? How do we know whether a given valuation model is more appropriate for a given company than the others? The answer is that we don't know for sure. Because valuation is an art all we have are broad guidelines which we can follow while selecting a given valuation model.

Let's look at some of those guidelines in this :

Characteristics of the Company:

The first and most important factor is the characteristics of the company that is being valued. Consider the fact that we can value a company like Ford Automobiles based on the amount of assets that they control. However, we cannot use the same technique to value a company like Google. Most assets controlled by Google are intellectual and intangible. If they are not complete they may have no use for the acquirer. Hence, the first factor that needs to be determined is whether the company can be subject to valuation based on its assets. If the company has assets that only they can acquire benefit from or if the assets are largely intangible, the asset valuation model needs to be ruled out.

Next, we also need to consider whether or not a company pays dividends. Utility companies for instance have always paid dividends and are likely to do so in the foreseeable future. On the other hand, companies like Microsoft have not paid dividends for a large part of their existence. Hence, while utility companies can be subjected to discounted dividends valuation, companies like Microsoft cannot be valued in the same manner.

Lastly, the purpose of the analysis must be clear to the person conducting the valuation exercise. The valuation for a short term investment will be different from a long term one. Hence, companies that have competitive advantage can be given a higher premium in the short run in the absence of any threat from the competition.

Characteristics of the Investor:

It may not seem that obvious, but the characteristics of the investor also play a big role in which model needs to be selected for valuation.

For instance, consider the case of a retail investor. A retail investor does have ownership of the asset. However, they do not have control over the assets. Hence, they are at the mercy of the dividend policy of the company and cannot predict their cash flows in any other manner. In this case, a discounted dividend approach may be more suitable as compared to other approaches.

Now, consider the case of an institutional investor. Institutional investors have deep pockets and are capable of buying a stake which is large enough to get the management to change the dividend payout policy. In this case, the discounted dividend model may not be very applicable. Instead what matters is the amount of free cash flow that can be generated by the company. Hence institutional investors tend to use discounted free cash flow models more often.

Lastly, if a competing firm makes an acquisition, then they can not only influence the dividend payout policy but the day to day functioning of the firm. Hence valuation here will be more accurate if the discounted residual income model is used.

Purpose of Investment:

Lastly, the purpose of investment also plays a major role in the valuation model being chosen.

For instance, consider the case when a conglomerate company makes an acquisition in an unrelated business. Here, the value derived by the investors will be directly related to the value of the assets themselves. The concept of synergy and the increase in value may not be applicable there. On the other hand, if a competing firm makes an acquisition, they can benefit from the economies of scale and other synergies that come with the acquisition of a business. Hence in this case the concept of synergy may also be applicable. Also, sometimes investors acquire private companies, only to make an exit by taking them public later on. In such case the valuation will totally depend on the retail investor's perception of value of that company. Hence, a different valuation model may have to be used.

Multiple Models:

An important point to note is that investors often use multiple models to derive the valuation of a company, instead of using a single model. The benefit of using multiple models is that the analyst can verify whether they are getting the same or similar measures of value from all models.

If the estimates are not similar, they will still gain a better understanding as to what the root cause of the higher valuation is and whether it is worth the additional premium. Hence, using multiple valuation models is always preferred to coming up with a valuation based on a single model.

Sum of the Parts Valuation

Equity valuation is usually conducted for an entire enterprise. For instance, if we are trying to come up with a valuation for Apple Inc, we will usually consider Apple Inc as being one single indivisible unit. This is because the cash flows that will accrue to Apple Inc are intertwined and all of the cash flows to the same company have almost the same level of riskiness.

This approach may be useful for companies which have one single business focus i.e. most of their business is concentrated in one industry only. An example would be Apple Inc which is largely involved in the consumer electronics industry.

However, it is not very useful for companies which have diverse business interests. For instance consider the case of Berkshire Hathaway which is the holding company headed by Warren Buffet. Berkshire Hathaway has business interests in insurance, railroads and even diary. Obviously the risks and rewards facing each business are very different. Hence, it would not be prudent to value the entire company as one indivisible unit. Rather, it would be more appropriate to value each line of business that the company has and then add these cash flows together to arrive at the final valuation.

This approach of conducting a valuation of individual lines of business and then adding these values to derive the corporate valuation is called the sum of the parts valuation approach. It may also be referred to as breakup value by many investors.

Closely linked to the idea of sum of the parts valuation is the idea of a conglomerate discount. The concept of conglomerate discount says that investors prefer companies which have a single minded focus i.e. they sell similar or related products. When companies diversify too much and enter into unrelated business, investors supposedly mark down the valuation of the company because of loss of focus. This markdown is called conglomerate discount.

Therefore, if a conglomerate has 3 lines of business A which is valued at Rs.10 million, B which is valued at Rs.25

million and C which is valued at Rs.15 million, then the ideal sum of the parts valuation should be Rs.50 million. However, conglomerate discount implies that the stocks of the combined entity will trade at an amount less than Rs.50 million, let's say Rs.47 million because investors are wary that the company is losing focus and may not excel at either of its businesses.

The idea that conglomerates do not perform as well as focused companies is grounded in a lot of research. Some of the factors which justify the existence of conglomerate discount are as follows:

- Conglomerates tend to have an inefficient internal capital allocation process. The limited resources at the disposal of the company may not be put to the best use. This is because in a conglomerate there is a lot of politicizing at the board level. Resources may therefore be allocated to the manager who has the most clout rather than the manager with the best project. Hence, it is hypothetically possible that Berkshire Hathaway may invest more money in its insurance company (GEICO) even though it would be clearly more profitable to invest in its railway company i.e. BNSF

- Secondly, if marketing gurus Al Ries and Jack Trout are to be believed, focusing on different businesses can lead to dilution of brand equity. Of course, the result is lower sales over a longer time horizon and finally the company may have to take a huge markdown on its equity valuation.

The existence of conglomerate discount is still a hotly debated topic. Some analysts argue that there is no discount as such and the company's are plain and simple undervalued in the market. However, other analysts argue that it has to be quite a coincidence that almost all the conglomerate companies are more or less undervalued in the market.

Either ways, as an analyst, we must be aware that unrelated businesses belonging to the same conglomerate can be valued using the sum of the parts valuation. Also, there is a possibility that the corporate value may be lower than the value reached by adding the individual parts. This could be caused by conglomerate discount.

Dividend Discount Model: Advantages

Dividend discount models are the first type of discounted cash flow models that we will study. The model simply discounts cash flows at a given rate just like any other DCF model. The difference lies in the fact that dividend discount models consider only "dividends" as being legitimate cash flows.

Therefore, if a firm pays no dividends at all, this model cannot be applied to the firm regardless of how profitable or cash flow efficient its operations are. This is one of the most popular models used to value businesses worldwide. The popularity stems from the fact that this model has some major advantages. The purpose of this is to discuss these advantages and bring to the student's attention, when this model will be useful.

Justification: The primary advantage of the dividend discount model is that it is grounded in theory. The justifications are rock solid and indisputable. The logic is simple. A business is a perpetual entity. When an investor buys a share of the business, they are basically paying a price today which entitles them to enjoy the benefits of all the dividends that the corporation will pay throughout its lifetime. Hence, the value of the firm is basically the value of a perpetual never ending stream of dividends that the buyer intends to receive later with the passage of time. Hence, many analysts believe that there is absolutely no subjectivity involved in this model and the logic is crystal clear.

Consistency: A second advantage of the dividend discount model is the fact that dividends tend to stay consistent over long periods of time. Companies experience a lot of volatility in measures like earnings and free cash flow. However, companies usually ensure that dividends are only paid out from cash which is expected to be present with the company every year. They do not set up unnecessarily high dividend expectations because not living up to those expectations makes the stock price plummet at a later date. Companies are very specific and announce any additional dividend as a one-time dividend.

No Subjectivity: There is no ambiguity regarding the definition of dividends. Whereas there is subjectivity as to what constitutes earnings and what constitutes free cash flow. Therefore, even if different analysts are asked to come up with a valuation for a company using a discounted dividend model, it is likely that they will come up with more or less the same valuation. This lack of subjectivity makes the model more reliable and hence more preferred.

No Requirement of Control: Dividends are the only measure of valuation available to the minority shareholder. While institutional investors can acquire big stakes and actually influence the dividend payout policies, minority shareholders have no control over the company. Thus, the only thing that they can be sure about is that fact that they will receive dividend year on year because they have been receiving it consistently in the past. Hence, as far as minority shareholders are concerned, dividends are really the only metric that they can use to value a corporation.

Mature Businesses: The regular payment of dividends is the sign that a company has matured in its business. Its business is stable and there is not much expectation of turbulence in the future unless something drastic happens. This information is valuable to many investors who prefer stability over possibility of quick gains. Thus, from a valuation point of view, it is far easier to arrive at a discount rate. Since consistency eliminates risk, dividends are generally discounted at a lower rate as compared to other metrics that can be used in valuation.

To sum it up, dividend discount models are preferred by two kinds of investor groups. One investor group consists of retail investors who prefer it because of their lack of control to influence the payout policies. The other investor group consists of risk averse investors who prefer it because of the stability and risk aversion which are built into this model.

Dividend Discount Valuation: H Model

The dividend discount model makes a lot of assumptions. Some of these assumptions are not considered to be viable by analysts. For instance, consider the assumption regarding growth rates. During the horizon period, the analyst estimates that the growth rate will be high, let's say 10% or 12%. Then, when the terminal value is to be calculated, the estimate if of a lower return that will continue till perpetuity. Let's say, a 5% rate is assumed.

To many critics, this seems like a critical flaw. They believe it to be an absurd assumption that a firm will make a 12% return in the 5th year and then suddenly the return will drop to 5% from the 6th year onwards. They believe that this assumption is absurd and use empirical analysis to prove that this is almost never the case.

Also, since the dividend discount model formula is extremely sensitive to assumptions regarding growth rates, they believe that the resultant valuation is quite a bit off the mark.

Therefore, to overcome this limitation, they have created a modified dividend discount model called the "H" model. In this , we will take a closer look at what the H model is all about.

The H Model:

The H model assumes that the earnings and dividends of the firm do not suddenly fall off a cliff when the horizon period ends. Rather, the decline in the growth rate is a gradual process. The assumption that the H model makes about this decline is that the decline is linear.

Hence instead of suddenly dropping from 12% to 5%, the growth rates will start declining from 12% at a given rate, let's say 10% every year. Hence, from 12% the rate will drop to 10.8% and then in the next period to 9.7% and so on. This decline would then continue until it reaches the long term growth rate of 5%. Once the 5% growth rate is reached, it stabilizes over there and remains in that state until perpetuity.

The Formula:

The derivation formula for calculating growth using the H growth rate requires some complex mathematics which is beyond the scope of this . Hence, for our understanding, let's just have a look at the formula and memorize it.

$$\text{Value of A Share (H Model)} = \frac{D0 * (1+gL)}{r-gL} + \frac{D0 * H * (gS-gL)}{r-gL}$$

where,

- D0 is the dividend received in the present year, let's assume the value to be Rs.25
- R is the rate of return expected by the investor, let's say 8% in this case
- gL is the long term growth rate i.e. 5% in this case
- gS is the short term growth rate i.e. 12% in this case

- H is the half-life of the high growth period i.e. our high growth period was 5 years, therefore the value of H is 2.5 for our purpose.

Calculation:

$$\text{Value of A Share (H Model)} = \frac{\text{Rs.}25*(1+0.05)}{0.08-0.05} + \frac{\text{Rs.}25 * 2.5 * (0.12-0.05)}{0.08-0.05}$$

= Rs.875 + Rs.145.833

= Rs.1020.33

Interpretation:

- The first component of the valuation i.e. Rs.875 in this case is what the value of the shares would be if there was no high growth period at all. Notice that the formula is quite similar to the Gordon Growth model formula

- The second component i.e. Rs.145.33 is the addition in value resulting from the high growth period for 5 years. This component is where the H model differs from other dividend discount models

Accuracy of the Model:

Empirical analysis has shown that the H model is most accurate when:

- The high growth period is shorter i.e. the model would be less accurate if we assumed a 20 year high growth period instead of a 5 year high growth period
- Also, the accuracy of the model increases when the spread between the long term growth rate and the short term growth rate is less

To conclude, the H model is a significant advancement in the field of equity valuation. It solves the problem of the abrupt decline in the growth rates that is assumed by the other models. However, it still provides only an estimate, albeit a better estimate than dividend discount models regarding the valuation of the stock.

Phases of Growth and Valuation Models

Dividend discount models are based on the assumption of constant or linear growth. However, a mere look at the empirical data will prove that this is not the case in reality. Growth is almost never linear or constant. In fact, in strategic management, the concept of product or company life cycle is taught wherein there are multiple phases of growth. It would be an irony if the management gurus preached the philosophy of multiple stages of growth while building companies but used the assumption of constant growth while valuing them. Therefore it is important to understand the different stages of growth as well as the valuation model that needs to be used at each stage.

Phase 1: Initial Growth Phase:

This is stage when the company has just come into existence or it has discovered a new product, market or technology that will form the basis of extraordinary growth in forthcoming years. This phase is characterized by high earnings which are driven by high profit margins. Also, since the company is experiencing immense growth it will need to build up more capacity. This requires initial capital investment and the free cash flow generated by the firm is negative. Therefore the dividend payouts are close to zero even though the return being earned by equity shareholders is higher than their expected rate of return.

Appropriate Valuation Model: Since the firm is at a very early stage and growth is likely to rise and fall over the next few years, a three stage dividend discount model should be used to accurately account for these changes in the process of valuation.

Phase 2: Transition Phase:

The transition phase happens when the product, market or technology introduced by the company is no longer innovative. Customers have become used to the product and competition has also increased. Thus the company experiences a slightly lower level of growth during this phase. This phase is characterized by earnings which are still above average but they are in a decline. This fall in earnings is caused by the reduced profit margins as a result of increased competition. However, at the same time the firm does not need massive influx of capital resources since the market is reaching closer to saturation and not much capital expenditure is required. Hence, the free cash flow from equity may be closer to zero or may even be slightly in the positive.

At this stage however, the firm may start paying off dividends since it is running out of opportunities to invest. This will also be characterized by a drop in the rate of return earned by equity shareholders.

Appropriate Valuation Model: Since not many changes are expected in the growth rate of the firm, the appropriate valuation model would be the two stage model. Dividends can be easily forecasted for a given horizon period and may stabilize over some time.

Phase 3: Maturity Phase

This is the stage when the industry has stabilized. The opportunities to grow are limited and consolidation takes place through mergers and acquisitions.

At the stage, most firms experience razor thin profit margins. However, the profits are stable and keep on flowing year after year in a very predictable manner. Also since there are almost no capital investments to be made, the firm experiences a massive positive cash flow to equity. Most of this cash flow is paid out to the shareholders in the form of dividends. However, the return on equity being provided to the shareholders may be very close to their required rate of return. Therefore, there are no abnormal returns being made at this stage.

Appropriate Valuation Model: At this stage, the simplistic assumptions of the Gordon growth model are more than sufficient to mimic the pattern of dividends that will be paid out by the firm. Hence, the valuation derived even from this simplistic elementary model is sufficient.

Companies may not necessarily go through all of these stages in the order mentioned. For instance, they may find new and new products to keep themselves in the growth stage for a longer time period. Consider the case of Apple which first introduced the iPod, followed by the iPhone and then the iPad to keep itself in the growth stage longer than any analyst had expected.

Dividend Discount Model: Share Repurchase Programs

In corporate finance we studied that companies had an option when it came to compensating their equity shareholders. They could both pay these shareholders cash dividends from the earnings of the current year or alternatively they could conduct a share repurchase program and buy back some shares from the same proceeds. The monetary effect would be the exact same. Differences, if any would arise because of the taxation policy of the particular country.

However, when it comes to valuation, there is a huge difference between cash dividends and share repurchase programs. However, some organizations prefer to conduct share repurchases. Hence, as an analyst it is important to understand how share repurchase affects the value of a company.

This explains the same in great detail:

Why Share Repurchase May Be Difficult To Value?

- Shares repurchase programs lead to a reduction in the number of shares outstanding. This is different because usually the number of shares remains constant. When the numbers of shares change, the "per share" valuation is also affected. This relationship is difficult to model and predict

- It is an unwritten rule, that dividends once announced should not be cut by the corporations. However, when it comes to share repurchases, there is no such rule. Companies do not find themselves under any obligation to conduct share repurchase year after year. Therefore, dividends are systematic and predictable whereas share repurchase may be erratic.

- There is almost always a direct correlation between earnings and dividend payout. This means that a higher profit automatically translates into a higher dividend. The same cannot be said about share repurchase. Share repurchase is driven by market price and the intention is to time the market. Hence companies may not indulge in share repurchase transactions even though they are flush with cash because they may believe that the share is overvalued at the current price. Once again, this creates unpredictability about the magnitude and timing of cash flows.

Therefore, share repurchase programs are not as reliable or as consistent as dividend payout programs. However, companies may indulge in these transactions and valuations have to be conducted.

How to Value Share Repurchases?

When dealing with share repurchase, the analyst may have to go beyond per share data. This is because the number of shares outstanding keeps on changing and hence per share data from last year may not be comparable to this year's numbers. Here are the steps commonly followed while valuing share repurchases:

- The total earnings of a company are first estimated. This is done in the same manner as it is done for dividend discount models
- The amount of earnings that are to be paid out to investors is then determined. Once again the payout ratio could be obtained empirically or based on specific information that a company may have on hand
- Thirdly, the market price of the shares outstanding at that time has to be forecasted. This is the difficult and subjective part. The bid that the company makes for its own shares has to be above the prevailing market price.

But estimating future prices is very difficult and is prone to a large degree of error.

- Lastly, using the amount of earnings to be distributed and the price per share, we can find out the number of shares that will be extinguished and therefore the new number of shares that will be outstanding.

- Once this is known, the valuation of these outstanding shares can also be derived.

To sum it up, the procedure largely depends on forecasting what the share price will be in the future. In the near future, an educated guess is still possible. However, predicting the stock price 5 or 10 years hence is sheer speculation and it is for this reason that analysts face problems arriving at a valuation for companies which use share repurchase as a tool to reward equity shareholders

Implied Dividend Growth Rate

We are now aware of the various models that are used for equity valuation like Gordon model, H model, 2 stage model etc. in each of these models, we were assuming that the given inputs are dividend, dividend growth rates and time horizon, The output that we expected from these models was the current stock price. While this is true most of the time, it may not always be correct.

The very same model that can be used to calculate share price can also be used in the reverse to figure out the rate of dividend growth that is being implied in the calculation. This may be a handy calculation to undertake. Let's have a closer look at this concept in this .

Backward Calculation:

The logic behind the calculation is simple. If all inputs except the growth rate are available then we can solve for the growth rate. This growth rate will be called the implied dividend growth rate as it is not directly mentioned. Instead it is included in the price. Instead of using the growth rate to move forward towards the share price, we can use the share price to move backwards towards the growth rate.

Sanity Check:

The implied dividend growth rate provides a great mechanism to check for sanity behind our assumptions and calculations. This is because it is empirically known that in the long run no company can grow at a rate which is much faster than the GDP. For instance, if the GDP growth is expected to be 4% over a long period of time, companies may grow at 3% of 6% i.e. one or two percentage points here and there.

However it would be downright impossible for any company to grow at 25% over an extended period of time when the GDP is growing at 4%. Hence if we take the current stock price from the market and solve for implied growth rate to find it at exorbitant levels like this, we immediately know that the share is overvalued. This provides an efficient sanity check mechanism and allows us to rule out obvious asset bubbles.

Calculation:

It is possible to calculate the implied rate of dividend growth, no matter which dividend discount model is being used.

- In case of Gordon model, the calculation is pretty straightforward. The formula can be easily remembered and is very convenient to use

- In case of H model, the formula becomes considerably more complex. To derive this formula, we will have to re-arrange the H model equation in such a way that r is on the left hand side and everything else is on the right hand side. This formula may be complex to remember. However, it is still easy to use and accurate.

- Lastly, in case of a multi stage dividend discount model, it becomes a little more difficult to apply this backward calculation. The formula is difficult to remember as well as difficult to use since it requires iterations to derive the correct answer.

The bottom line, therefore is that regardless of the type of model that has to be used, backward calculations are possible. Also, it does make sense to conduct these calculations. It reveals one of the fundamental assumptions built in the market price and therefore reveals its sanity!

Sustainable Growth Rate: Concept

We have studied the various discounted cash flow valuation models in this module. These different models need to be applied in different situations. We have studied these situations as well. However, regardless of which model is being applied, one thing remains constant.

In the end, the growth rate of the company plateaus down at a certain level. It can continue at this rate forever, meaning that it is "sustainable". Now, since terminal value is the most important component of valuation and since sustainable growth rate is an important determinant of terminal value, we need to understand the concept of sustainable growth rate in detail.

This will explain this concept of sustainable growth rate in detail.

What is Sustainable Growth Rate?

In jargonized terms, sustainable growth rate is the rate at which the earnings and dividends of any firm can continue to grow indefinitely. The implicit assumption behind sustainable growth rate is that no new debt or equity is being issued and that the capital structure of the firm remains unchanged.

In this case, the sustainable growth rate possible in any organization remains a simple function of the proportion of earnings that are retained and reinvested in the business as well as the returns that can be generated from those earnings. Simply put:

Sustainable Growth Rate = b * ROE

Where,

b = the reinvestment rate which is being followed by the organization

ROE is the Return on Equity which is earned by the organization

Why Is It Important To Calculate Sustainable Growth Rate?

The calculation of sustainable growth rate is important because it answers two very important questions:

1. It lets the analysts and the investors know the maximum possible rate at which the organization can grow. This is under the assumption the no additional funding is being raised either by debt or by equity

2. Secondly, this rate also provides an estimate when it comes to raising external capital. It provides a guideline as to how much funds should be obtained and on what terms.

Sustainable growth rate is basically a link between the nature of the current operations of a firm and its future valuation.

Example:

To understand the concept of sustainable growth rate better, let's have a look at an example.

Let's say that a company pays out 40% of its earnings as dividends each year. Also, historically it has been making a stable return on equity at 15%. What is the sustainable growth rate for this company?

Answer:

Since the company pays out 40% of its earnings as dividends, it is implied that it retains the balance 60% for reinvestment. Hence b = 0.6 i.e. 60%. At the same time, ROE is stated to be 15%.

Therefore, the sustainable growth rate which the company can finance through its internal accruals is 15% *0.6 = 9%.

Hence with this capital structure and this dividend policy, the company can continue to grow at the rate of 9% forever.

Interpretation:

Now, since we know the sustainable growth rate, how do we include it in our decision making? Here is an example for the same:

- **Growth rate expected to be greater than sustainable growth rate:** Let's say that the company is expecting to grow at 14% for the next few years. However, its sustainable growth rate shows that it can sustain only 9% if its policies remain unchanged. This analysis will provide a clear indication to the management that their plans are off base when compared to reality. To grow at 14% given the current scenario, the company would have to reduce dividends, raise more capital or both.

This analysis provides a double checking mechanism for checking the validity of the future plans of the company

- **Growth rate expected to be lesser than sustainable growth rate:** On the other hand, let's say given the current market condition, the management foresees that the organization will only be able to grow at the rate of 7%. However, the sustainable growth rate analysis suggests that 9% growth is possible given the current policy. In such a case, management may decide to increase their dividend payouts.

Hence, the bottom line is that a comparison between the sustainable growth rate and the expected future growth rate provides guidelines based on which policies pertaining to raising capital and changing the dividend payout must be built.

Dividend Discount Model: Disadvantages

The dividend discount model also has its fair share of criticism. While some have hailed it as being indisputable and being not subjective, recent academicians and practitioners have come up with arguments that make you believe the exact opposite. Recent studies have unearthed some glaring flaws in what was considered to be a perfect valuation model. This is focused on understanding these shortcomings. This knowledge will help us understand when not to apply the dividend discount model.

Limited Use: The model is only applicable to mature, stable companies who have a proven track record of paying out dividends consistently. While, prima facie, it may seem like a good thing, there is a big trade-off. Investors who only invest in mature stable companies tend to miss out high growth ones. High growth companies, by definition face lots of opportunities in the future. They may want to develop new products or explore new markets. To do so, they may need more cash than they have on hand. Hence such companies have to raise more equity or debt. Obviously they cannot afford the luxury of having the cash to pay out dividends. These companies are therefore missed by investors who are focused too much on the dividends.

For instance, investors following the dividend discount model would never have invested in companies like Google of Facebook. Even, a global behemoth like Microsoft did not have any track record of paying dividends until very recently. Hence, according to dividend discount model, these companies cannot be valued at all!

Many investors prefer an alternate approach. They try to forecast the time when the growing company will actually evolve into a mature stable business and will start paying out dividends. However, this is extremely difficult. The projections become more and more risky as we try to project farther and farther into the future. Thus, we can conclude that the dividend discount models have limited applicability.

May Not Be Related To Earnings: Another major disadvantage is the fact that the dividend discount model implicitly assumes that the dividends paid out are correlated to earnings. This means that higher earnings will translate into higher dividends and vice versa. But, in practice, this is almost never the case. Companies strive to maintain stable dividend payouts, even if they are facing extreme variations in their earnings. There have been instances where companies have been simultaneously borrowing cash while maintaining a dividend payout. In this case, this is a clear incorrect utilization of resources and paying dividends is eroding value. Hence, assuming that dividends are directly related to value creation is a faulty assumption until it is backed by relevant data.

Too Many Assumptions: The dividend discount model is full of too many assumptions. There are assumptions regarding dividends which we discussed above. Then there are also assumptions regarding growth rate, interest rates and tax rates. Most of these factors are beyond the control of the investors. This factor too reduces the validity of the model.

Tax Efficiency: In many countries, it may not be efficient to pay dividends. The tax structures are created in such a way that capital gains may be taxed lower than dividends. Also, many tax structures may encourage repurchase of shares instead of paying out dividends. In these countries most of the companies will not pay out dividends because it leads to dilution of value. Any investor who only strictly believes in dividend discount model will have no option but to ignore all the shares pertaining to that particular country! This is one more reason why dividend discount model fails to guide investors.

Control: Lastly, the dividend discount model is not applicable to large shareholders. Since they buy a big stake in the corporation, they have some degree of control and can influence the dividend policy if they want to. Thus, for them, at least, dividends are an irrelevant metric.

Therefore, dividend discount model is not very useful for investors who want to invest in high risk return companies. Also, it may not be in alignment with the tax structures being followed by certain countries.

Single Period Dividend Discount Model

To understand the dividend discount model, we need to start from the basics. The simplest way to understand the dividend discount model and its application is to first start with a single period and then later extend it on to more complex cases. Hence, the term single period dividend discount model.

The objective of application of this model is to derive what the fair market price of the stock should be if we know certain other information about that stock. The other information is the expected future price, expected dividend payout in that single period and the investors required rate of return.

Let's understand the application of a single period dividend discount model with the help of an example:

Example:

An investor is wondering what the correct price of a share should be? He knows that his required rate of return is 9%.

He also knows that the share will give a Rs.5 dividend in the current period and the expected market value at the end of the period is Rs.200. What would the fair price for such a stock be?

Calculation:

We know that the value of the stock is equal to the present value of all the future cash flows that can be derived from it. In this case we are getting cash flows in two different forms. One form is dividends and the other form is the final sale proceeds.

Let's call the dividends D1 and the final sale proceeds P1. Thus the total cash flow that we will obtain at the end of the period is D1+P1. Now the next task is to calculate the present value of these cash flows i.e. discount them at the expected rate of return for the investor.

Hence, the formula pertaining to single period dividend discount model is:

Present Market Price = (D1+P1)/(1+r)

Therefore, in our case, it equals:

(Rs.5+Rs.200)/1.09 = Rs.188.07

Thus, the fair market value of this stock should ideally be Rs.188.07

Interpreting the Results:

In case the investor is fairly confident about all of his/her assumptions then the stock will provide them with a value equal to Rs.188.07 in present value terms.

- Hence, if the price is values at Rs.188.07, the investor may or may not buy the stock. Since it just meets the investor's expectations, there are no abnormal profits to be made
- In case, the price is less than Rs.188.07, then the stock is undervalued and the investor should immediately make the purchase. If the investor's assumptions are correct, he/she stands to make a windfall gain from the buying and selling of this stock
- In case, the price is greater than Rs.188.07, then the investor should refrain from making the purchase. The stock is intrinsically worth less than what the investor would pay off for it and the investor would be better off putting that money in another investment.

Difficulty in Implementation:

The single period dividend model can tell you whether a price is overvalued or undervalued if two variables which will become known only in the future i.e. the future price and the future dividend are accurately predicted today!

Also, while theoretically investors are supposed to know their required rate of return, not many investors actually do! So the third variable being used in the formula is also slightly difficult to predict.

Needless to say, this is not a very good idea. Guessing an accurate dividend itself may be difficult. However, guessing an accurate future price is almost impossible! Therefore, it may seem like this model is not very useful and it really isn't if you consider it on its own.

However, this model forms the building block for later models some of which are based on more realistic assumptions and are therefore much more applicable and helpful.

Two Period Dividend Discount Model

The next step towards understanding the dividend discount model is to extend the conclusions derived from the single step dividend model. This brings us to the two period dividend discount model. In this model we will use the same logic. However, we will extend the assumption regarding the holding period. Instead of selling his stock at the end of period 1, the investor holds on to the stock and only sells it at the end of period two. The question arises, how the investor should value the stock this time.

Once again, we will understand this with the help of an example:

Example:

An investor is confident that a certain stock can be sold off for Rs.100 if it is held on to for 2 years. He has a required rate of return of 10%.He is also confident that the company will pay a Rs.4 dividend in the first year and a Rs.6 dividend in the second year. However, he is not certain about what the price of the stock should be today?

Calculation:

Once again, the value of the stock is only equal to the present value of all future cash flows that can be derived from that stock. In this case, we will receive three different cash flows.

- The first cash flow is dividend 1. Let's call it D1
- The second cash flow is dividend 2. Let's call it D2
- Lastly, the third cash flow is the final selling price i.e. P2

Also, note that the first cash flow will be received at the end of year 1. However, the second and third cash flows will be simultaneously received at the end of year 2.

Hence, we will discount the first dividend of Rs.4 at 10% for 1 period only. However, second dividend plus the final sale proceeds i.e. Rs.6 and Rs.100 are to be received after two years, therefore they will be discounted for 2 periods.

The formula for the two period dividend discount model is:

$$= [D1/(1+r)] + [D2+P2/(1+r)2]$$
$$= [Rs.4/(1.1)] + [Rs.6+Rs.100/(1.1)2]$$
$$= Rs.3.7 + Rs.87.6$$
$$= Rs.91.3$$

Thus, from the given assumptions the value of this investment should be equal to Rs.91.3 in present value terms

Interpretation:

Once again,

- If the current market price is Rs.91.3, the investor should be indifferent
- If the current market price is less than Rs.91.3, the investor should buy the share as it is undervalued

- If the current market price is greater than Rs.91.3, then the investor should not buy the share as it is overvalued

Difficulties in Implementation:

This model too cannot be used on its own for very accurate results. Once again the reason is that it uses hard to predict variables like future price and future dividends as inputs. However, the two step dividend discount model is proof that the concept of discounting dividends can be extended to several years.

This proof will be used in the next , to finally arrive at the generic dividend discount model. The assumptions in the generic model are comparably more realistic which makes it usable. In fact it is amongst the most preferred equity valuation models used by cautious investors.

Dividend Discount Generic Model

we saw how information regarding the possible future price, dividends and rate of return expected by the investor can be used to derive the present value of an equity security. However, these models were limited in their scope.

Firstly, they had limited horizon periods viz. one period and two periods. Secondly, they required an estimate of the future stock price which is almost impossible to predict.

In this , we will use the former two models to come up with the generic dividend discount model. This model can value equity securities given the infinite and perpetual life that they have. Also, it does not require an estimate of the selling price.

Instead the estimate of the selling price is replaced by the concept of terminal value. Let's have a look at these concepts in greater detail in this .

The concept of terminal value:

The generic dividend discount model disregards the idea of selling price and the resulting capital gain as being a part of the valuation of any given stock. The logic behind this is that if A sells his stock to B, then the buying price that B will pay to A will also be in anticipation of future dividends.

Thus, there is no selling price or P1 as we have considered in the previous. P1 is the price received by A, if you think from the point of view of A. Rather we have to think in terms of the security itself. The intrinsic value of the security is not driven by the selling price. There is no reason why selling price should even exist!

The selling price is thus nothing more than the discounted present value of future dividends that B is paying to A to collect the dividends himself later. Thus, it can be said that the value of a stock is derived only and only on the basis of the dividends that it pays out through its lifetime. The value of a stock is therefore the value of a perpetual stream of dividends that are expected to be received.

This makes things easier from a practical point of view as well. Dividends that will be paid out by the firm are relatively easier to predict. Hence, the valuation can be more accurate. Instead if we use expected future price of a stock to be a factor in valuing the stock, we are stuck into a circular loop. Any valuation becomes purely a judgment call.

The Formula:

The valuation of a stock can therefore simply be reduced to being the present value of all future dividends that will be received by the company.

Thus, if the company is going to live for "n" years, then the value of this stock will be:

$Value = (D1/(1+r)1) + (D2/(1+r)2) + (D3/(1+r)3) \ldots\ldots (Dn/(1+r)n)$

This is the gist of the dividend discount model. The earlier proved the fact that a stock could be valued if it's selling price and dividends were known. This proves that selling price itself is nothing but the present value of dividends. Hence, the value of any stock, according to this model depends upon the future stream of dividends that can be derived from it.

Horizon Period and Terminal Value:

For the purpose of valuation, the calculation is broken down into two parts. One part is called the horizon period. The analyst can choose the length of the horizon period as per his/her liking. Analysts usually choose 5 to 7 years as the horizon period. For the horizon period, the dividends are explicitly projected and discounted to reach the value.

On the other hand, the rest of the stocks dividends are valued as perpetuity. This perpetuity is called the terminal value. The value of the stock is thus composed of the value of the horizon period as well as the terminal value.

The dividend discount model is one of the oldest models for stock valuation. All other models are derivations or offshoots of this fundamental model.

Dividend Discount Model: Gordon Growth Rate

In the previous, we became aware that the value of a stock can be split into two parts. One part is the horizon period i.e. the period chosen by the analyst for which they believe they can accurately forecast the financials of the company and therefore its dividends. This part remains the same when the calculation is done as per Gordon Growth model as well.

The second part is the terminal value. This is where the Gordon growth formula becomes important. The Gordon growth model simply assumes that the dividends of a stock keep of increasing forever at a given constant rate. Let us understand this with the help of an example.

Example:

Let's say that an analyst wants to forecast the value of a given stock. He is using the dividend discount model to do so. He selects a 5 year horizon period for which he will project the most accurate possible dividend projections. Beyond that he will consider the stock to be perpetuity.

Calculation under Dividend Discount Model:

Let's assume that the firm will pay dividends of Rs.4, Rs.5, Rs.6, Rs.7 and Rs.8 in each of the 5 years of the horizon period. The normal dividend discount model will assume that the firm will continue paying, let's say Rs.10 dividend from the 6th year to perpetuity. This means that the dividends being forecasted are constant.

Calculation under Dividend Discount Model using Gordon Growth Rate:

In this case too, we will assume that the firm pays 4, Rs.5, Rs.6, Rs.7 and Rs.8 in each of the 5 years of the horizon period. This is the part where both the models remain the same. However, instead of assuming that the dividend from 6th year onwards will remain constant at Rs.10, the Gordon growth model assumes that the dividend will keep on increasing at a constant rate. So, if this rate was 10%, then the dividend for the 7th year will be Rs.11 and that of the 8th year will be Rs.12.21. It then calculates the terminal value as a growing perpetuity instead of it being an ordinary perpetuity. This assumption is obviously more viable given the fact that dividends do actually grow year on year. Hence, instead of assuming that they will stop growing instantly we can assume that they will grow at a given constant rate till eternity.

The Gordon Growth Formula:

According to the Gordon growth model, the value of the stock is derived from two parts:

Value = Present Value of Horizon + Terminal Value

The terminal value is then calculated as a growing perpetuity. There is some complex mathematics behind the derivation of this formula. However, that is not what we are concerned with.

The formula simply is:

Terminal Value = $(D1/(r-g))$ where:

- D1 is the dividend expected to be received at the end of Year 1
- R is the rate of return expected by the investor and
- G is the perpetual growth rate at which the dividends are expected to grow

Calculation:

For instance, in the above case, the terminal value can be calculated as follows, if the rate of return expected by the investors is 12%

$D1$ = Rs.11, r = 12% and g = 10%

Therefore, the terminal value for the above stock is Rs.550

Important Point to Note:

The Gordon model only works if the rate of return expected by the investors i.e. r is greater than the constant growth rate that is assumed by the investor i.e. "g" . Hence, r always has to be greater than g. g could even be a negative number implying that dividends are declining at a steady rate. However, it cannot be equal to or greater than r.

Also, not that we did not take the first value from the terminal period i.e. the dividend of 6th year i.e. Rs.10. For our purpose, that should be considered D0. We need to use the value of the second dividend that is paid in the terminal period i.e. D1. Alternatively, we could use $D0*(1+g)$ which is the same thing as D1

Gordon Growth Model: Pros and Cons

The Gordon growth model is a well known and widely known model for valuing equity securities. However, as with every model, there are some pros and cons that need to be understood before this model is applied. Understanding of these pros and cons will help differentiating between situations wherein it would be prudent to apply the Gordon growth model and situations wherein that would not be the case.

The points in favor of the Gordon growth model i.e. the pros have been listed first:

- **Simplicity:** The Gordon growth model is extremely simple to explain and understand. It does not take too much intelligence to assume that the dividends are expected go an increasing at a constant rate. This simplicity is what makes this model widely understood and therefore widely used. More complex models have been proposed in place of the Gordon model. But the Gordon model has stood the test of time, because it mimics the dividend pattern exhibited by most companies and it does so while maintaining it's simplicity.

- **Reverse Logic:** Gordon growth model need not be applied only to find the correct intrinsic value of the share. Instead, given the current share price, a reverse analysis can be conducted and the growth rate being implied in the current market price can be found out. This helps in stating facts in a manner which is intuitively understandable. For instance, if the result of this backward analysis is that the dividends are expected to grow 20% year on year forever, then we know that this is not possible and the firm is overvalued. When the whole economy grows at an average of 3% to 5% per annum, how can a single firm continue to grow at 20% forever?

- **Scope:** The Gordon growth model is applicable to most companies, especially if the company has a relatively mature and stable business. Also, the Gordon growth model can be used to find out if the indices are valued correctly or whether the market is amidst a bubble.

At the same time, the points against Gordon growth model i.e. the cons are as follows:

- **Precision Required:** The Gordon growth model is highly sensitive to changes in inputs. For instance if you change the required rate of return (r) or the constant growth rate (g) even a little bit, then there will be a huge change in the resultant terminal value and therefore the value of the stock. Hence, for the model to be accurate, the inputs have to be forecasted very accurately. The problem is that these inputs cannot be forecasted with a great degree of precision by investors.

As such the Gordon growth model is susceptible to the "garbage in garbage out" syndrome. Even if slightly inaccurate assumptions are used, the results will be way off the mark!

- **Non Linear Growth Patterns:** Also, the Gordon growth model assumes a constant growth rate. This makes the growth of the company's dividends appear linear. In reality, empirical evidence has proven that dividend growth is seldom linear. The reason behind this is the existence of business cycles. During boom times, companies experience a surge in earnings and pay out generous dividends and during lean times they pay out lesser dividends. Of course, companies make an attempt to smoothen out these dividend payments. However, it is difficult if not impossible. Even the American telecom giant (AT&T) which has always been known for its impeccable dividend payouts had to cut dividends when it fell on rough times. Thus, the dividend payouts are non-linear to say the least and Gordon growth model may not be the best approximation.

To conclude, it would be apt to say that Gordon growth model has more pros than cons. Analysts must be careful to avoid the pitfalls associated with the use of the model. Overall, it is a handy tool to estimate the value of equity of any company.

Valuing Preference Shares Using Dividend Discount Model

The dividend discount model is also used to measure the value of preference equity in addition to forecasting the value of ordinary equity. There are certain assumptions and clarifications that need to be made regarding the use of dividend discount model for valuing preference equity. The purpose of this is to provide this information in an easy to understand manner.

Preference Shares: Recap

Just to remind the readers, preference shares are securities which can be thought of as being mid-way between debt and equity. Preference shareholders do not get a variable return. Rather they get a fixed rate of return like debt holders. Thus it does not face the risks of an equity shareholder and also does not get the slow return of a bond holder. It is somewhere in between these two extremes.

This is because payments to preference shares are not legally mandatory. If the company makes a profit, they must receive their fixed dividend before the ordinary shareholders are paid.

Implications:

These defining characteristics of preference shares lead to certain implications. They are as follows:

- Dividends, in case of preference shareholders are fixed. Hence, there need not be any speculation as to what the pattern of dividend payouts will. Whether, it will be constant as in the case of the dividend discount model or whether they will grow at a constant rate like in Gordon growth model. The cash flow timings and amounts are almost certain in case of preference shares

- The only risk factors that need to be considered are whether the firm has an option to call the preference shares back and extinguish them. Also, if the firm does not make a profit in any given year, then the preference shareholders will not get paid.

Valuation of a Preference Share:

The valuation of preference shares is a very straightforward exercise. Usually preference shares pay a constant dividend. This dividend is the percentage of the face value of the share. For instance, a preference share with the face value of Rs.100 which pays 5% dividend will pay Rs.5 in dividends.

Hence, if the required rate of return of an investor is 10%, then the value of the preference share can be arrived at using the simple formula

Value (Preference Share) = D/r

Where,

D is the constant dollar amount of dividends being received

And r is the required rate of return for the investor

Hence, the value of this preference share would be Rs.5/0.1 = Rs.50

Assumptions:

The risks that the firm can call the bonds back or the profits may not be paid as preferred dividends in a certain year have not been considered in this formula. Hence, if any of these risks is foreseeable, the value derived from the formula i.e. Rs.50 in this case, needs to be reduced to account for that risk.

- The value of the call option can be derived from option pricing models like binomial model, black schools model etc. The value of the preferred share should be adjusted since the buyer of the preferred share is also acting as seller of the call option to the company
- Also, if the analyst forecasts, that some dividends may not be paid out in the future, then they must subtract the present value of the missed dividend from the present value of the preference share.

Conclusion:

A plain vanilla preference share can be easily valued using the dividend discount model. A plain vanilla preferred share is nothing but perpetuity! For more exotic and complex types of preference shares, the initial value is derived from the model and then adjustments are made to account for the risks that have been missed out.

Link between Present Value of Growth Opportunities (PVGO) and Dividend Valuation

Valuing a corporation is a complex exercise. This is partly because there are multiple ways of looking at the same information. One such example is mentioned in this . Dividend discount valuation and present value of growth opportunities may seem to be two completely different topics. However, there exists a link between them. In fact if the dividend discount valuation is known, we can point out with some degree of precision what is the amount of money that the acquirer is paying anticipating growth opportunities in the target firm.

A Different Perspective:

Let's say that we have used the dividend discount model and come to the conclusion that a certain company is worth Rs.100. We done this by adding the present value derived from the horizon periods to the terminal value which could have been derived using the Gordon growth model.

Hence, Value (Firm) = Present Value (Horizon Period) +Terminal Value

Now, a different way to look at this would be to consider the value of the company in two parts again. One part would be the value that the firm would have if it simply continued its current level of operations and paid out all its earnings as dividend i.e. the no growth scenario

The residual part would therefore be the present value of the anticipated gains from growth in the firm's business. To put it in the form of a formula:

Value (Firm) = Value (No Growth Assumption) + Value (Growth Opportunities)

Now, if we just rearrange the components of the formula, we get

Present Value (Growth Opportunities) = Value (Firm) – Value (No Growth Assumption)

In this case, we already know the value of the firm i.e. Rs.100. So, if we can find the value of the firm without the growth, we can obtain the present value of growth opportunities.

Finding the Value of a Firm with No Growth Assumption

To answer this question, we need to think about how does a firm which is not aiming for any growth functions. Well, it gives out 100% of its earnings as dividend and does not invest anything in growth. Hence, the earnings will be the same every year and there will be no growth.

Value (No Growth Assumption) = Earnings/Required Rate of Return

Usually, earnings and dividends mean two very different things. However, in this case, they mean the exact same thing because the firm is paying 100% of its earnings out as dividends.

Since, we know the present dividend, we can solve for the value of the firm with no growth assumption. Let's say this value is Rs.45

Hence, the present value of growth opportunity being paid by the firm is Rs.100 - Rs.45 i.e. Rs.55

Use of this Analysis:

This analysis is widely used within to industry to double check whether the price being paid for the target firm is rational. For instance, let's say if in this case, the target firm is a market leader with 60% market share. We are paying over two times the amount that the firm is worth considering its current operations and assets.

However, since the firm already has 60% market share, it is highly unlikely that the firm will able to grow twice as big unless the market itself is growing rapidly and the firm is expected to get a large share of that growth.

Thus, we must acquire this firm at Rs.100 only if we are sure that it is worth Rs.55 in terms of future opportunities i.e. the assets or the operations which are not present as of now.

Conclusion:

The job of an analyst is to check multiple times using different relationships amongst the financial statements and common sense whether the price being paid is fair.

Sustainable Growth Rate: Concept

We have studied the various discounted cash flow valuation models in this module. These different models need to be applied in different situations. We have studied these situations as well. However, regardless of which model is being applied, one thing remains constant.

In the end, the growth rate of the company plateaus down at a certain level. It can continue at this rate forever, meaning that it is "sustainable". Now, since terminal value is the most important component of valuation and since sustainable growth rate is an important determinant of terminal value, we need to understand the concept of sustainable growth rate in detail.

This will explain this concept of sustainable growth rate in detail.

What is Sustainable Growth Rate?

In jargonized terms, sustainable growth rate is the rate at which the earnings and dividends of any firm can continue to grow indefinitely. The implicit assumption behind sustainable growth rate is that no new debt or equity is being issued and that the capital structure of the firm remains unchanged.

In this case, the sustainable growth rate possible in any organization remains a simple function of the proportion of earnings that are retained and reinvested in the business as well as the returns that can be generated from those earnings.

Simply put:

Sustainable Growth Rate = b * ROE

Where,

b = the reinvestment rate which is being followed by the organization

ROE is the Return on Equity which is earned by the organization

Why Is It Important To Calculate Sustainable Growth Rate?

The calculation of sustainable growth rate is important because it answers two very important questions:

1. It lets the analysts and the investors know the maximum possible rate at which the organization can grow. This is under the assumption the no additional funding is being raised either by debt or by equity

2. Secondly, this rate also provides an estimate when it comes to raising external capital. It provides a guideline as to how much funds should be obtained and on what terms.

Sustainable growth rate is basically a link between the nature of the current operations of a firm and its future valuation.

Example:

To understand the concept of sustainable growth rate better, let's have a look at an example.

Let's say that a company pays out 40% of its earnings as dividends each year. Also, historically it has been making a stable return on equity at 15%. What is the sustainable growth rate for this company?

Answer:

Since the company pays out 40% of its earnings as dividends, it is implied that it retains the balance 60% for reinvestment. Hence b = 0.6 i.e. 60%. At the same time, ROE is stated to be 15%.

Therefore, the sustainable growth rate which the company can finance through its internal accruals is 15% *0.6 = 9%.

Hence with this capital structure and this dividend policy, the company can continue to grow at the rate of 9% forever.

Interpretation:

Now, since we know the sustainable growth rate, how do we include it in our decision making? Here is an example for the same:

- **Growth rate expected to be greater than sustainable growth rate:** Let's say that the company is expecting to grow at 14% for the next few years. However, its sustainable growth rate shows that it can sustain only 9% if its policies remain unchanged. This analysis will provide a clear indication to the management that their plans are off base when compared to reality. To grow at 14% given the current scenario, the company would have to reduce dividends, raise more capital or both.

This analysis provides a double checking mechanism for checking the validity of the future plans of the company

- **Growth rate expected to be lesser than sustainable growth rate:** On the other hand, let's say given the current market condition, the management foresees that the organization will only be able to grow at the rate of 7%. However, the sustainable growth rate analysis suggests that 9% growth is possible given the current policy. In such a case, management may decide to increase their dividend payouts.

Hence, the bottom line is that a comparison between the sustainable growth rate and the expected future growth rate provides guidelines based on which policies pertaining to raising capital and changing the dividend payout must be built.

Sustainable Growth Rate and the Du-Pont Analysis (PRAT Model)

We now have a basic understanding of the concept of sustainable growth rate and how it related to the valuation of any given firm. In this , we will dig deeper in the same formula in an attempt to connect it with the famous Du-Pont model which is used worldwide to predict the Return On Equity or the ROE number.

Let's look at this concept in greater detail in this :

The Sustainable Growth Rate Formula:

The sustainable growth rate formula is pretty straightforward. It is derived based on two factors. One of those factors is the retention rate of earnings or "b" and the other is the Return on Equity or ROE. Hence, the ROE number is an important determinant of the formula.

However, in real life, it is very difficult to predict what the ROE number for the future periods will be. It is for this reason that Du-Pont analysis had been created in the first place. Since ROE is a determinant of the sustainable growth rate, Du-Pont analysis is also intertwined with the concept of sustainable growth rate. This will explain the correlation

Breaking Down the ROE – The PRAT model:

The formula for sustainable growth rate is

SGR = b * ROE

Where b represents the retained earnings i.e. (net income – dividends)/ net income And ROE represents the return on equity which can be broken down into its 3 component ratios with the Du Point analysis

$$SGR = \frac{(net\ income - dividends)}{Net\ income} \times \frac{(net\ income)}{Sales} \times \frac{(Sales)}{Total\ Assets} \times \frac{(Total\ assets)}{Equity}$$

We can see that the Du-Pont analysis has been further developed in this model. Just like the Du-Pont ratio is internally made up of 3 ratios, similarly the sustainable growth rate ratio is also internally made up of 4 ratios viz, P, R, A and T

Where:

P represents profit margin

R represents retention rate

A represents Asset Turnover

And surprisingly T represents Financial Leverage

Note that leverage is not represented by L. Rather it is represented by T

Example:

If a company has a profit margin of 14%, asset turnover of 2, leverage ratio of 1/2 and pays out 60% of its earnings as dividends, then what is the rate at which this company can grow indefinitely?

Answer:

Since 60% of the earnings are paid out, the balance 40% are retained.

Therefore SGR = 14% * 0.4 *2 *0.5

= 5.6%

Hence as per the above inputs the company can continue to grow at a rate of 5.6% indefinitely. However, obviously the underlying assumption states that the capital structure policy and the dividend policy remain unchanged!

The PRAT model is important from an exam point of view. This is because it helps us calculate the Sustainable Growth Rate even though the components of sustainable growth rate may not be explicitly stated in the question paper.

Analysis: The Financing Factors:

From an analysis point of view, we can see that two out of the four factors in the PRAT model are directly linked to the financing policy of the company. These two factors are retention rate and asset turnover. Thus, while creating the financing policy companies must take into account the fact that they could be changing the valuation of their firm for better or for worse.

However, since these factors are within the direct control of the company, the prediction pertaining to these two components shows less error and tends to be more accurate.

The Performance Factors:

The other two factors viz. the profit margin and the asset turnover are performance driven. This means that they are not under the direct and unilateral control of the organization. There are factors beyond the reach of the company which can affect these components of the ROE and hence the sustainable growth rate number. The predictions pertaining to these components have a higher possibility of error and hence less accuracy.

Dividend Discount Valuation: H Model

The dividend discount model makes a lot of assumptions. Some of these assumptions are not considered to be viable by analysts. For instance, consider the assumption regarding growth rates. During the horizon period, the analyst estimates that the growth rate will be high, let's say 10% or 12%. Then, when the terminal value is to be calculated, the estimate if of a lower return that will continue till perpetuity. Let's say, a 5% rate is assumed.

To many critics, this seems like a critical flaw. They believe it to be an absurd assumption that a firm will make a 12% return in the 5th year and then suddenly the return will drop to 5% from the 6th year onwards. They believe that this assumption is absurd and use empirical analysis to prove that this is almost never the case.

Also, since the dividend discount model formula is extremely sensitive to assumptions regarding growth rates, they believe that the resultant valuation is quite a bit off the mark.

Therefore, to overcome this limitation, they have created a modified dividend discount model called the "H" model. In this , we will take a closer look at what the H model is all about.

The H Model:

The H model assumes that the earnings and dividends of the firm do not suddenly fall off a cliff when the horizon period ends. Rather, the decline in the growth rate is a gradual process. The assumption that the H model makes about this decline is that the decline is linear.

Hence instead of suddenly dropping from 12% to 5%, the growth rates will start declining from 12% at a given rate, let's say 10% every year. Hence, from 12% the rate will drop to 10.8% and then in the next period to 9.7% and so on. This decline would then continue until it reaches the long term growth rate of 5%. Once the 5% growth rate is reached, it stabilizes over there and remains in that state until perpetuity.

The Formula:

The derivation formula for calculating growth using the H growth rate requires some complex mathematics which is beyond the scope of this . Hence, for our understanding, let's just have a look at the formula and memorize it.

$$\text{Value of A Share (H Model)} = \frac{D0 * (1+gL)}{r-gL} + \frac{D0 * H * (gS-gL)}{r-gL}$$

where,

- D0 is the dividend received in the present year, let's assume the value to be Rs.25
- R is the rate of return expected by the investor, let's say 8% in this case
- gL is the long term growth rate i.e. 5% in this case
- gS is the short term growth rate i.e. 12% in this case
- H is the half-life of the high growth period i.e. our high growth period was 5 years, therefore the value of H is 2.5 for our purpose.

Calculation:

$$\text{Value of A Share (H Model)} = \frac{Rs.25*(1+0.05) + Rs.25 * 2.5 * (0.12-0.05)}{}$$

$$\frac{}{0.08-0.05} \qquad \frac{}{0.08-0.05}$$

= Rs.875 + Rs.145.833

= Rs.1020.33

Interpretation:

- The first component of the valuation i.e. Rs.875 in this case is what the value of the shares would be if there was no high growth period at all. Notice that the formula is quite similar to the Gordon Growth model formula

- The second component i.e. Rs.145.33 is the addition in value resulting from the high growth period for 5 years. This component is where the H model differs from other dividend discount models

Accuracy of the Model:

Empirical analysis has shown that the H model is most accurate when:

- The high growth period is shorter i.e. the model would be less accurate if we assumed a 20 year high growth period instead of a 5 year high growth period

- Also, the accuracy of the model increases when the spread between the long term growth rate and the short term growth rate is less

To conclude, the H model is a significant advancement in the field of equity valuation. It solves the problem of the abrupt decline in the growth rates that is assumed by the other models. However, it still provides only an estimate, albeit a better estimate than dividend discount models regarding the valuation of the stock.

Phases of Growth and Valuation Models

Dividend discount models are based on the assumption of constant or linear growth. However, a mere look at the empirical data will prove that this is not the case in reality. Growth is almost never linear or constant. In fact, in strategic management, the concept of product or company life cycle is taught wherein there are multiple phases of growth. It would be an irony if the management gurus preached the philosophy of multiple stages of growth while building companies but used the assumption of constant growth while valuing them. Therefore it is important to understand the different stages of growth as well as the valuation model that needs to be used at each stage.

Phase 1: Initial Growth Phase:

This is stage when the company has just come into existence or it has discovered a new product, market or technology that will form the basis of extraordinary growth in forthcoming years. This phase is characterized by high earnings which are driven by high profit margins. Also, since the company is experiencing immense growth it will need to build up more capacity. This requires initial capital investment and the free cash flow generated by the firm is negative. Therefore the dividend payouts are close to zero even though the return being earned by equity shareholders is higher than their expected rate of return.

Appropriate Valuation Model: Since the firm is at a very early stage and growth is likely to rise and fall over the next few years, a three stage dividend discount model should be used to accurately account for these changes in the process of valuation.

Phase 2: Transition Phase:

The transition phase happens when the product, market or technology introduced by the company is no longer innovative. Customers have become used to the product and competition has also increased. Thus the company experiences a slightly lower level of growth during this phase. This phase is characterized by earnings which are still above average but they are in a decline. This fall in earnings is caused by the reduced profit margins as a result of increased competition. However, at the same time the firm does not need massive influx of capital resources since the market is reaching closer to saturation and not much capital expenditure is required. Hence, the free cash flow from equity may be closer to zero or may even be slightly in the positive.

At this stage however, the firm may start paying off dividends since it is running out of opportunities to invest. This will also be characterized by a drop in the rate of return earned by equity shareholders.

Appropriate Valuation Model: Since not many changes are expected in the growth rate of the firm, the appropriate valuation model would be the two stage model. Dividends can be easily forecasted for a given horizon period and may stabilize over some time.

Phase 3: Maturity Phase

This is the stage when the industry has stabilized. The opportunities to grow are limited and consolidation takes place through mergers and acquisitions.

At the stage, most firms experience razor thin profit margins. However, the profits are stable and keep on flowing year after year in a very predictable manner. Also since there are almost no capital investments to be made, the firm experiences a massive positive cash flow to equity. Most of this cash flow is paid out to the shareholders in the form of dividends. However, the return on equity being provided to the shareholders may be very close to their required rate of return. Therefore, there are no abnormal returns being made at this stage.

Appropriate Valuation Model: At this stage, the simplistic assumptions of the Gordon growth model are more than sufficient to mimic the pattern of dividends that will be paid out by the firm. Hence, the valuation derived even from this simplistic elementary model is sufficient.

Companies may not necessarily go through all of these stages in the order mentioned. For instance, they may find new and new products to keep themselves in the growth stage for a longer time period. Consider the case of Apple which first introduced the iPod, followed by the iPhone and then the iPad to keep itself in the growth stage longer than any analyst had expected.

Dividend Discount Model: Share Repurchase Programs

corporate finance we studied that companies had an option when it came to compensating their equity shareholders. They could both pay these shareholders cash dividends from the earnings of the current year or alternatively they could conduct a share repurchase program and buy back some shares from the same proceeds. The monetary effect would be the exact same. Differences, if any would arise because of the taxation policy of the particular country.

However, when it comes to valuation, there is a huge difference between cash dividends and share repurchase programs. However, some organizations prefer to conduct share repurchases. Hence, as an analyst it is important to understand how share repurchase affects the value of a company.

This explains the same in great detail:

Why Share Repurchase May Be Difficult To Value?

- Shares repurchase programs lead to a reduction in the number of shares outstanding. This is different because usually the number of shares remains constant. When the numbers of shares change, the "per share" valuation is also affected. This relationship is difficult to model and predict

- It is an unwritten rule, that dividends once announced should not be cut by the corporations. However, when it comes to share repurchases, there is no such rule. Companies do not find themselves under any obligation to conduct share repurchase year after year. Therefore, dividends are systematic and predictable whereas share repurchase may be erratic.

- There is almost always a direct correlation between earnings and dividend payout. This means that a higher profit automatically translates into a higher dividend. The same cannot be said about share repurchase. Share repurchase is driven by market price and the intention is to time the market. Hence companies may not indulge in share repurchase transactions even though they are flush with cash because they may believe that the share is overvalued at the current price. Once again, this creates unpredictability about the magnitude and timing of cash flows.

Therefore, share repurchase programs are not as reliable or as consistent as dividend payout programs. However, companies may indulge in these transactions and valuations have to be conducted.

How to Value Share Repurchases?

When dealing with share repurchase, the analyst may have to go beyond per share data. This is because the number of shares outstanding keeps on changing and hence per share data from last year may not be comparable to this year's numbers. Here are the steps commonly followed while valuing share repurchases:

- The total earnings of a company are first estimated. This is done in the same manner as it is done for dividend discount models

- The amount of earnings that are to be paid out to investors is then determined. Once again the payout ratio could be obtained empirically or based on specific information that a company may have on hand

- Thirdly, the market price of the shares outstanding at that time has to be forecasted. This is the difficult and subjective part. The bid that the company makes for its own shares has to be above the prevailing market price. But estimating future prices is very difficult and is prone to a large degree of error.

- Lastly, using the amount of earnings to be distributed and the price per share, we can find out the number of shares that will be extinguished and therefore the new number of shares that will be outstanding.

- Once this is known, the valuation of these outstanding shares can also be derived.

To sum it up, the procedure largely depends on forecasting what the share price will be in the future. In the near future, an educated guess is still possible. However, predicting the stock price 5 or 10 years hence is sheer speculation and it is for this reason that analysts face problems arriving at a valuation for companies which use share repurchase as a tool to reward equity shareholders

Implied Dividend Growth Rate

We are now aware of the various models that are used for equity valuation like Gordon model, H model, 2 stage model etc. in each of these models, we were assuming that the given inputs are dividend, dividend growth rates and time horizon, The output that we expected from these models was the current stock price. While this is true most of the time, it may not always be correct.

The very same model that can be used to calculate share price can also be used in the reverse to figure out the rate of dividend growth that is being implied in the calculation. This may be a handy calculation to undertake. Let's have a closer look at this concept in this .

Backward Calculation:

The logic behind the calculation is simple. If all inputs except the growth rate are available then we can solve for the growth rate. This growth rate will be called the implied dividend growth rate as it is not directly mentioned. Instead it is included in the price. Instead of using the growth rate to move forward towards the share price, we can use the share price to move backwards towards the growth rate.

Sanity Check:

The implied dividend growth rate provides a great mechanism to check for sanity behind our assumptions and calculations. This is because it is empirically known that in the long run no company can grow at a rate which is much faster than the GDP. For instance, if the GDP growth is expected to be 4% over a long period of time, companies may grow at 3% of 6% i.e. one or two percentage points here and there.

However it would be downright impossible for any company to grow at 25% over an extended period of time when the GDP is growing at 4%. Hence if we take the current stock price from the market and solve for implied growth rate to find it at exorbitant levels like this, we immediately know that the share is overvalued. This provides an efficient sanity check mechanism and allows us to rule out obvious asset bubbles.

Calculation:

It is possible to calculate the implied rate of dividend growth, no matter which dividend discount model is being used.

In case of Gordon model, the calculation is pretty

straightforward. The formula can be easily remembered and is very convenient to use

- In case of H model, the formula becomes considerably more complex. To derive this formula, we will have to re-arrange the H model equation in such a way that r is on the left hand side and everything else is on the right hand side. This formula may be complex to remember. However, it is still easy to use and accurate.

- Lastly, in case of a multi stage dividend discount model, it becomes a little more difficult to apply this backward calculation. The formula is difficult to remember as well as difficult to use since it requires iterations to derive the correct answer.

The bottom line, therefore is that regardless of the type of model that has to be used, backward calculations are possible. Also, it does make sense to conduct these calculations. It reveals one of the fundamental assumptions built in the market price and therefore reveals its sanity!

Spreadsheet Modeling: Dividend Discount Model

In the past, we have studied about the various models that are available to help us predict the value of a firm based on the dividends that it provides. However, all these models had one flaw. They expected that the dividends of the firm will follow some set pattern. For instance, the assumptions were that that the dividend of a firm will continue to rise for 5% for the next 3 years.

Now, the reasons behind these assumptions were twofold. Firstly, dividends are difficult to predict. Hence, assuming a pattern reduces the risk of making mistakes. Thus, the ease of forecasting is one of the reasons. Also, calculations related to valuation of stocks have to be conducted at a fast pace. Hence, the formulas assume simplistic patterns in which dividends are expected to behave in the future. This is for calculation ease.

However, both the forecasting ease and the calculation ease make the formula less effective and less accurate. Therefore, in real life, analysts almost always use more complex tool like spreadsheet models to come up with a more accurate valuation.

Real Life Scenarios Are Complex:

Real life scenarios are much more complex. Almost no company is able to follow a predictable pattern when it comes to making dividend payments. Companies may experience a 5% growth this year but may soon experience a 3% decline the next year. Multiple factors like macro-economy, the nature of competition, the changing purchasing powers etc determine the stability of the dividends. For most companies, these factors will not be stable and hence their dividends are unlikely to match the trends which are built in any of the formulas.

Valuation Is Sensitive To Inputs:

Some degree of error is always present in all calculations. If the error is small then the effort required to correct it may not be worth the while. However, valuation models are extremely sensitive to changes in inputs. This is because they are calculating values of cash flows over a very long period of time. Hence, the inputs need to be perfect and errors cannot be ignored. Thus analysts simply cannot work with the suboptimal results that the formula provides and a better mechanism is required.

Infinite Possibilities Can Be Built In:

This is where spreadsheet modeling comes to the rescue. Spreadsheet tools have advanced calculation capabilities. They can process millions of bits of data and provide the relevant answer in a few seconds. Also, spreadsheet modeling allows separating the inputs from the calculations. Thus, scenario analysis can be conducted with extreme ease and in a matter of minutes.

Scenario Analysis:

Scenario analyses have become more and more important in the recent past. Analysts and investors have realized that it is almost impossible to predict the exact movement in the valuation of a company. Hence, instead of looking for one value, they are usually looking at a range of values. These ranges provide a more accurate estimate of what the future is expected to be like. It is here that scenario analysis helps a lot. Analysts can vary the inputs in different combinations and note down the effect of the change in these inputs in the valuation of the firm.

Sensitivity Analysis:

While conducting the scenario analysis, analysts can also understand the relationship between individual inputs and the valuation derived. In some cases, growth rate may be the most important factor whereas in other cases the discount rate may be of more importance. Either ways, spreadsheet models help uncover these relationships in real time with almost no effort. In conclusion, it needs to be understood that there is really nothing that cannot be done manually which the spreadsheet models do for us. Spreadsheet models just help us to automate the whole process and increase the speed at which these calculations can be conducted. But, in the financial markets, speed is what is of utmost importance and hence spreadsheets have become an integral part of the business.

Any analyst who wishes to have a fruitful career in finance ought to be aware of and skilled in the use of spreadsheets to create financial models.

Estimating Future Dividends

We have discussed various types of dividend payout models. We have discussed the Gordon growth model, the H model, one stage, two stage, multi-stage and even spreadsheet models. These models are varied in their approach towards calculating the value of a firm. Yet the common link amongst these models is the fact that they all use probable future dividends as inputs to derive the value of the firm as an output. So in a way, the estimate of future dividends is the fuel that powers all these models. It may therefore be worthwhile to understand what are the techniques used to arrive at these future projections.

There are multiple ways in which analysts can estimate the probable future dividends. Some of them have been listed down in this .

Dividend Payout Ratio:

Dividend payout ratio is the ratio between the amount of book profits that a company has generated and the amount of cash it is paying off as dividends. Many companies maintain their dividend payouts as a percentage of their earnings because earnings somehow are supposed to indicate the value creation that the firm has done in a given period.

Thus, if an analyst knows the firm's target dividend payout ratio, they can then calculate the expected profits which they can then further use to extrapolate what the dividends in future periods are likely to be. Let's have a look at some sources that analysts can use to obtain this information.

- **Notes:** The firm's target dividend payout ratio is often mentioned in the footnotes that accompany the financial statements. In fact it is provided with the sole objective of helping the analysts to calculate the probable value of future dividends and value the firm.

- **Filings:** In many cases, the firm may not explicitly mention the quantum of dividend that they intend to pay. In such cases, empirical evidence can be used to derive a reasonably accurate value. Empirical data can be obtained from the firm's previous filings with the stock exchanges.

- **Management Discussions:** Lastly, many times analysts directly schedule calls with the management to obtain information which may help them value the firm. In such calls, the issue of dividend payout ratio is often discussed. Firm's however, are very cautious before they make any promises pertaining to dividend payouts to the investors. Failure to meet these promises often results in a sharp decline of the value of the stock.

Dividend per Share:

Another chain of thought recommends that the dividend payout ratio is not that helpful if the number of shares amongst which the dividend has to be distributed keeps on changing. The firm may maintain a stable payout ratio but by changing the number of shares outstanding, they can change the amount of dividend that will be received by the investors. Hence, dividend per share is the more accurate metric. Once again analyst calls, empirical data or public announcements from the company can be used to derive this value.

Direct Calculation:

Lastly, many analysts prefer not to extrapolate future dividends from any other metric. To calculate the amount of dividends that can be paid out, they first calculate the amount of free cash flow that the firm may have on hand. Then they consider other factors like stage of growth, condition of the macro-economy, competition etc and arrive at an estimate of the amount of dividends that are expected to be paid out. Needless to say, that this calculation is complex and requires deep understanding of the company's business environment. Hence this method is used quite rarely.

Conclusion:

To sum it up, projecting future dividends can be done in a myriad of ways. Each way presents a different level of tradeoff between the quality of the estimate and the ease with which it can be calculated. However, dividends being more stable than other metrics, analysts often obtain accurate estimates regardless of the method that they use for their calculation.

Dividend Discount Models: Some Points to Consider

Dividend discount models are amongst the oldest category of valuation models that have been used by the market. However, there are some peculiar characteristics of this model that should be considered before deciding whether or not to use this model. These characteristics have been mentioned in this .

Long Term View:

Dividend discount models are only meant for investors who want to invest long term in the growth of a company. The model is not known for beating the market every year. This is not the investing strategy that you would want to use if your intent is to flip stocks quickly. In fact, most stocks recommended by dividend discount models are known to remain low priced for a few years before the market corrects itself and shares return to their fair value.

Studies have shown that if the return of shares selected using dividend discount models is compared to the general market over a short time period, these shares almost never outperform the market. However, if the time horizon is changed from months to years, these shares do the exact opposite and almost always outperform the market. Hence dividend discount models are for what Warren Buffet likes to call "decades investors" or people who have no intention of pulling out their money for a decade or so.

Hence, it is recommended only to seasoned investors who have a lot of patience, are not in the habit of checking their stock price daily and ascertaining the change in value and have the cash flow ability to bear what is "perceived loss" till they make abnormal gains. If investors using dividend discount models face monetary pressures, they may have to liquidate their holding at an unfavorable time which obviously is not a desirable outcome.

Biased Towards Certain Stocks:

Secondly, dividend discount models are heavily biased towards only one kind of stocks. This flaw is basically built into the model. The model divides the infinite life of the company into two parts. One is the horizon period and the second is the perpetuity. Horizon periods are estimated to have a higher growth rate. Thus the model pays more attention to the earnings and dividends that will be paid in the near future. Dividend discount models are notorious because they always recommend the same kind of stock i.e. the one with low price to earnings ratio and high dividend yields.

Analysts have conducted studies wherein they found out that the stocks recommended after conducting an elaborate dividend discount model analysis were the exact same if only two parameters were used i.e. low price to earnings ratios and high dividend yields.

The disadvantage of picking these types of shares is that investors may miss out on multi-bagger stocks which do not have these characteristics but give handsome payoffs to investors who are willing to take the risks.

Tax Disadvantage:

Lastly, stocks following dividend discount models have a strong disadvantage in many countries. In many countries, dividends are taxed at two levels. Also, in many countries the rate at which corporations are taxed for paying dividends is higher than if the use other methods like share repurchase. However, this tax disadvantage built into the dividend discount models is offset by the security that a stable stream of predictable cash flows provides. So ultimately, it becomes a matter of perspective. Some investors prefer tax efficient companies whereas others prefer consistent payouts and are willing to pay a price for the same.

The dividend discount models are believed by many investors to be the gold standard in investing. As we can see that is not the case. Dividend discount models are the gold standard for a certain type of investors. Hence before applying the principles, one must be aware of the probable outcome that they can expect.

Concept of Free Cash Flow

Introduction: Concept of Free Cash Flow

We have already established that it is cash and not earnings, which is important when it comes to the valuation of any company. In the previous module, we assumed that cash flow was equivalent to the dividends received by investors. This point of view was based on what seems like an obvious fact that investors pay cash in the form of stock price and receive cash only in the form of dividends. Hence, dividends are pretty much the sole source of cash inflow.

However, a little logical reasoning proves this chain of thought to be flawed. There can be other sources of receiving cash apart from dividend payments. Let's have a look at that reasoning first.

Dividends Are Not The Only Source of Investor Compensation:

If dividends are the only source of inflow for the investor, then companies that never pay dividend should have no value at all! However, they do have value. The reason behind this is pretty simple.

Dividends only determine the time when the cash will be released to investors. Once the company has made money, it doesn't matter if it pays dividends today or if it pays them tomorrow with interest as compensation.

Thus, if a company has created value, its share price will go up regardless of whether it is paying dividend right away or will do so at a later date. According to most experts, it is cash flow or more specifically "free cash flow" which tells us whether or not a company has created value. Let's look at this concept of free cash flow in more detail.

The All Important "Free Cash Flow"

Many experts including Warren Buffet believe that accounting statements are not useful when it comes to valuing a company. They simple see a company as a cash processing machine.

On one hand, it guzzles cash in the form of investments whereas on the other hand, it gives out cash in the form of revenues and profits. Therefore, as long as the company can produce more cash than it consumes, it is creating value.

The cash flow situation of a company can be measures through multiple metrics. However, as investors we are concerned with two particular matrices called the free cash flow to the firm and free cash flow to equity.

Free Cash Flow To Firm:

Free cash flow to the firm, as the name suggests, is the amount of cash flow that is available to all the investors of the firm. This cash flow figure is arrived at after making multiple adjustments.

- First, all operating expenses have to be subtracted. It is assumed that these expenses are being paid in cash
- Then, cash is set aside for short term investments in working capital and inventory for the forthcoming cycle
- Lastly, big capital investments, if any are made from this cash flow and hence these amounts also need to be deducted

It is important that these issues are prioritized in the order in which they have been mentioned above. At the end of all the planning and future investments, the company will be left with some cash for which it has no immediate use. This is called "Free cash flow to the firm"

On a technical note, the FCFF is available to both equity as well as debt investors. However, in reality debt investors have a preferential claim on the cash flow.

Free Cash Flow To Equity:

Now, the FCFF amount pertains to all investors in the company. However, the first right to that cash belongs to the debt holders. After financing obligations are fulfilled, it is the preference shareholders who get a claim on that money.

Lastly after everyone else is paid off, the residual free cash flow belongs to the equity shareholder. This is Free Cash Flow to Equity or FCFE i.e. the second cash flow metric that is commonly used.

Free cash flow to equity is a closer proxy for dividends than free cash flow to the firm. This is because the firm pays dividends only after the other investors have been paid off.

Why Is Free Cash Flow Approach Better Than Dividend Discount Models?

The dividend discount models assume that the investors have no control over the payout policy of the firm whatsoever. This is true for the case of the minority shareholder. Hence, it is said that as far as the minority shareholder is concerned, dividend discount models may be the best tools for valuing a firm.

This may not be the case when potentially bigger shareholders come into picture. Bigger shareholders find the free cash flow approach much more suitable for their needs. Thus free cash flow approach is said to have the perspective of a big ticket acquirer.

In this , we will compare the dividend discount model and the free cash flow model.

Dividends Do Not Mean Good Performance:

The dividend discount models use dividends as a proxy for the firm's operating performance. The underlying logic is that a firm can continue to pay dividends in the long run only if its underlying business is stable and prosperous. Multiple cases in the stock market have shown that this need not necessarily be the case. Firm's can borrow money and keep on paying dividends and mask the fact that the underlying business is rapidly deteriorating. Alternatively, firms could have robust business models and may need cash to invest in them and hence may feel that paying out dividends is sub-optimal utilization of cash.

The correlation between dividends and underlying performance is just that, a correlation! Dividends are neither the cause nor the effect of good performance.

It just happens to be the case that a lot of good businesses tend to pay dividends too! Dividends are just used to distribute the wealth. They are in no way, signals that wealth has been created by the company.

Free Cash Flow Means Value Creation:

Free cash flow, on the other hand, is an almost certain signal that the firm is in good financial health. A firm cannot free cash flow by borrowing more money or by creating fictitious accounting entries. For free cash flow to be present the operations have to be efficient and the firm has to be creating value.

The presence of free cash flow therefore is a huge positive signal. The absence may not be considered to be a sure shot negative thing. When companies are in their growth phase, they need cash. Hence, in such scenarios the present day free cash flow may be negative. However, it is expected to be much better in the future.

Thus, free cash flow as a metric, provides a much deeper insight into the workings of a firm.

Control Perspective:

Also, dividend discount models have the perspective of a minority shareholder who has no control over the proceedings. They have no option but to agree to the diktat of the board of directors. On the other hand, larger shareholders may be able to purchase a significant holding which might put them in a position to control or at least influence the decisions of the board of directors. They may therefore be able to get a payout policy passed which may be as per their convenience.

For larger shareholders, dividends are completely irrelevant. Neither do they signal a firm's underlying performance, nor are they the only way that they as investors can plow back their cash.

Difficult To Predict:

All being said, the free cash flow models also have a major disadvantage. This disadvantage is that free cash flow is very difficult to predict. While dividends are completely in the hands of the management and can be accurately estimated based on empirical evidence, free cash flow is influenced by numerous factors and predicting it is a challenge to say the least. However, the challenge is worthwhile since a more accurate valuation is derived using this model.

Lastly, in some cases there may be a huge difference in the valuation derived from dividend discount models and from free cash flow models. Smaller differences can simply be ignored. However, when differences are large, they may be because of the control premium that some large investors are willing to pay.

Free Cash Flow to the Firm vs. Free Cash Flow to Equity

Free cash flow models can be further categorized into two types. There are certain kinds of models which pertain to free cash flow that the firm as a whole will generate whereas there are others that pertain solely to the perspective of equity shareholders.

These models are quite different from each other. It is therefore essential to understand, when and under what circumstances is one model a better choice than the other. This will explain the difference between these two types of free cash flow models:

Free Cash Flow To The Firm:

- **Interpretation:** This is the amount of cash flow which is available to all the investors of the firm which would typically include bondholders as well as shareholders. The cash flow being considered here is operating cash flow and is generated by using the operating assets of the firm. If there are other assets like cash, marketable securities or any other kind of investments which are not used in day to day operations, their discounted present value needs to be added separately to the value of the firm as they are not considered in the free cash flow to the firm metric.

- **Discount Factor:** Since the cash flow in FCFF pertains to the entire firm, it must be discounted at the weighted average cost of capital i.e. WACC. The idea is that the costs of debt and equity must be combined in the exact proportion in which they are being used. Also, tax benefits arising because of usage of debt are to be considered.

- **Formula:** The formula for calculating the value of the firm using FCFF approach is as follows:

Value (Firm) = Σ FCFF/ $(1+(WACC))^{\wedge n}$

Free Cash Flow To Equity:

- **Interpretation:** Free cash flow to equity is the amount of cash flow that accrues to equity shareholders after all the operating, growth, expansion and even financing costs of the company have been met. Since this is the amount which is expected to be paid to equity shareholders, the value of equity shares can be directly calculated using these values.

- **Discount Factor:** Since FCFE pertains only to equity shareholders, it needs to be discounted at a rate which reflects its level of risk. The risk of being an equity shareholder is higher than the risk of the entire firm if the firm is leveraged. Thus, the appropriate discount factor for these cash flows will be expected return on equity.

- **Formula:** The value of a firm's equity can be calculated in one of these two ways:
    1. By discounting all the future free cash flows to equity at return on equity.

        Value (Firm's Equity) = ΣFCFE/ (1+(Return on Equity))^{n}
    2. By subtracting the discounted present value of debt from the discounted present value of the firm.

Value (Firm's Equity) = Value (Firm) − Value (Firm's Debt)

Thus, it is possible to calculate the value of the firm's equity by an indirect route even if we are not aware of what the free cash flows to that firm's equity shareholders will be.

Important:

- *FCFF calculates the total value of the firm whereas FCFE calculates the value of the firm's equity. In a levered firm, the value of a firm's equity is a subset of the total value of the firm. **Thus they are not two different methods to calculate the same output! The output derived from discounting FCFF is the firm's value whereas that derived from discounting FCFE is the value of the firm's equity.***
- FCFF must be discounted at the weighted average cost of capital i.e. WACC whereas FCFE must be discounted

at the expected cost of equity. Discounting the wrong cash flow with the wrong discount factor will obviously lead to a wrong valuation!

Calculating Free Cash Flow to Firm: Method #1 (Contd): Treatment of Fixed Capital Expenditure

In the previous we learned that free cash flow to the firm is closely related to the concept of cash flow from operations. The major difference was in the way free cash flow to the firm (FCFF) treats long term capital expenditures versus how they get treated in the regular cash flow statement.

The regular cash flow statement does not include long term capital expenditures in cash flow from operations. Rather, it includes this cash outflow in another section called cash flow from financing. The reason is that the objective is to find out the cash flow that the firm generates from its day to day operations.

However, when it comes to free cash flow to the firm the objective has changed. The objective is no longer concerned with whether the cash flow is generated from regular operating activities or from one off transactions. The objective here is to find out what is the amount of free cash flow that the shareholders of the firm will be left with at the end of the given year. Hence, in this case long term capital expenditures are included in the calculation.

This may seem like a very small difference. However, wrongly including or excluding the fixed capital expenditure is a mistake that most students make. Hence, in this we will discuss in detail about how fixed capital needs to be treated while calculating the free cash flow to the firm.

Gross Fixed Capital Expenditure vs. Net Fixed Capital Expenditure:

Firstly, we need to clarify the concepts of gross fixed capital expenditure and net fixed capital expenditure. We intuitively know the difference between gross and net. The same logic can be applied here as well.

Gross fixed capital expenditure includes only the additions that have been made to the fixed capital in a particular accounting period. These additions could arise because of purchase of new fixed capital. Also, they could arise because of addition of improvements or repairs to the existing fixed capital which has been capitalized in the balance sheet. Hence, when it comes to "gross", we are considering only the outflow.

Net, fixed capital expenditure, on the other hand also includes the inflows. For instance, it is possible that we may have sold some of the machinery that we have in this given year. In this case, there will be a positive inflow of cash. Hence, we must reduce our outflow by that amount to arrive at the net cash flow on capital expenditure.

Let's understand this with the help of an example:

If we purchase a machine worth Rs.100 in the present year and at the same time sell a machine for Rs.20 in the same year, then:

Gross Fixed Capital Investment is Rs.100

Whereas Net Fixed Capital Investment is, Rs.100 - Rs.20 i.e. Rs.80

It is the net fixed capital investment that we are concerned with while calculating free cash flow to the firm. Hence, if we are given cash inflows and outflows separately, we need to arrive at the net figure before we can begin our calculations.

Given the above concepts, there are three possible cases that may arise. Let's see how we must deal with them:

Case #1: No Sale of Fixed Assets

In a given period, there could be only additions to the amount of fixed assets and no subtractions i.e. no sale. This is an easy case since here gross fixed capital investment equals net fixed capital investment. We can simply use this number during our calculation of free cash flow to the firm.

Case #2: Sale of Fixed Assets

The second case is simple too. In this case, we are given the cash proceeds from sale and the cash outflow from purchase directly. In this case, we can just subtract the numbers like in the above example and arrive at the net fixed capital investment figure that we need.

Remember, this number could be positive, negative or zero!

Case #3: Sale of Fixed Assets (Indirect Derivation)

The complicated case is when the cash proceeds and the cash outflow numbers are not directly given. In such cases, we need to calculate the net cash flow from fixed capital investment in the following manner:

1. First, we need to see the difference between the opening and the closing amounts of fixed assets listed on the balance sheet. The first step is to derive the change in the fixed assets in the current year by using the formula:

   Change in Fixed Assets: Closing Balance – Opening Balance

2. We need to adjust this change for the gain or loss that was made by selling old assets. This gain or loss is not reflected on the balance sheet. Instead it is reflected on the income statement. Therefore, we need to subtract the gain and add the loss. So now, our formula is modified to

   Change in fixed Assets: Closing Balance – Opening Balance – Gain + Loss

3. Lastly, if the depreciation for the asset sold is separately mentioned and we haven't accounted for it, we must also add this to our calculation. Ensure that you haven't already added this depreciation earlier to avoid double counting. So, our final formula is:

   Change in Fixed Assets: Closing Balance – Opening Balance – Gain + Loss + Depreciation

   This calculation is the most difficult part in deriving free cash flow to the firm. A good conceptual understanding is recommended for this part to avoid errors.

Calculating Free Cash Flow to the Firm: Method #2: Cash Flow From Operations

Now, it's time to move on to the second metric which can be used to derive the free cash flow to the firm (FCFF). This metric is the cash flow from operations. These types of questions involve a complete cash flow statement being provided as the question and expect the student to derive free cash flow to the firm (FCFF) as an output.

The conceptual understanding that we built in the previous regarding the difference between these two closely related terms will come in handy here.

The Difference Is Net Cash Flow towards Long Term Investments:

We already know that the difference between free cash flow to the firm (FCFF) and cash flow from operations arises because we consider long term investments as being the part of one whereas we do not consider for the other. Therefore, simply put, free cash flow to the firm (FCFF) can be derived from cash flow from operations in the following manner:

Free Cash Flow to the Firm (FCFF) = Cash flow from Operations – Net Investment in Long Term Assets

However, this is only an approximation. To consider this to be the accurate derivation of free cash flow to the firm (FCFF) would be an oversimplification.

The Complication: Interest Expense:

There is another complication that is introduced because of the way we treat interest expense while preparing statement of cash flows.

We consider interest expense as a financing expense. That is because, the operating cash flows of the firm would remain the exact same regardless of whether we ran the business on own money or on borrowed money. Hence, we subtract them from operating cash flow and send them to financing cash flows.

Well, when calculating free cash flow to the firm (FCFF) the perspective changes. We are not concerned whether the money is spent because of regular operations or not. All we are concerned about is that it reduces the money available for the investors. Hence, we must add this interest expense back our above formula. Thus we arrive at a modified formula which is

FCFF = Cash flow from Operations – Net Investment in Long Term Assets + Interest Expense

However, adding back the entire interest expense would also be an oversimplification. Thus, we have one last adjustment to make before we can arrive at the free cash flow to the firm (FCFF) number. That adjustment pertains to tax. Since we have already deducted tax, the interest expenditure should be reduced to account for its effect. Thus the final formula is:

FCFF = Cash flow from Operations – Net Investment in Long Term Assets + Interest Expense (1-Tax Rate)

The above two formulas were only intermediate calculations to derive the final formula and must not be used. The third formula (highlighted with border) is the final formula which must be used to derive the free cash flow to the firm in case all the inputs are known.

Example:

Let's understand this with the help of an example:

Cash flow from operations = Rs.1000

Cash Outflow (New Machine) = Rs.250

Cash Inflow (Sale of Old Machine) = Rs.75

Interest Expense = Rs.100

Tax Rate = 40%

Calculation #1: *Net Cash Flow towards Long Term Assets = Rs.250 - Rs.75 =* ***Rs.175***

Calculation #2: *After Tax Interest Expense = Rs.100*(1 – 0.40) =* ***Rs.60***

Therefore,

FCFF = Cash flow from Operations – Net Investment in Long Term Assets + Interest Expense (1-Tax Rate)

FCFF = Rs.1000 – Rs.175 + Rs.60 =Rs.885

Needless to say this is an over simplified version for explanation. The questions on the exam will be much more detailed and calculation intensive. However, the logic and the steps required to solve them remain the same.

Source of Confusion:

Many students find it confusing that interest is the only financing expense that is added back to cash flow from operations. They wonder why other expenses like dividends and share repurchases do not affect the free cash flow to the firm.

The answer lies in the sequence in which the calculation happens. Interest expense was earlier subtracted to arrive at the net income. Hence, it needs to be added back. Other expenses like dividends and share repurchase are not subtracted to arrive at the net income and hence no adjustments need to be made for them!

Calculating Free Cash Flow to Firm: Method 3: EBIT

In the previous, we learned about how to calculate the cash flow from operations if the cash flow statement or the income statement were given in the question paper. In many cases, these financial statements may not be given in full in the question paper.

Instead, some excerpts from these statements may be provided in the question paper. One such example is when Earnings before Interest and Taxes (EBIT) is provided. Hence, we have to begin our calculation with EBIT and derive the free cash flow to the firm based on the supplementary information. This will describe this process in detail.

It is important to understand the logic behind the formulas. Mindless rote learning of the formula may cause the students to forget the formulas or get confused. If the concepts are clear, students can derive the formulas themselves as and when required.

Here is a step by step procedure to calculate the free cash flow to the firm from EBIT.

Step 1: Add Back Depreciation:

Depreciation is a non cash expense. It has been reduced from the revenues to arrive at EBIT. Hence, to derive what the true cash flow of the firm is, we need to add back the depreciation amount. This is the standard procedure we use while preparing any cash flow statement.

Step 2: Adjust EBIT for taxes

Step 2 is where things get slightly complicated. Now, notice the fact that we are working with EBIT which is earnings before interest and taxes. This means that we haven't accounted for interest as well as taxes and their effects on the cash flow.

Interest does not have any effect on the cash flow. We haven't subtracted it from EBIT and hence there is no need to add it back.

Taxes on the other hand are a different matter. They are a cash outflow which occurs at a later stage in the income statement. Hence, while deriving free cash flows to the firm we must adjust the EBIT for taxes. This is done by subtracting the tax amount from EBIT.

For example, the EBIT was Rs.1000 and there was a 40% tax rate. At a later stage on the income statement, the company will pay 40% of this Rs.1000 as cash flow. Hence, its EBIT will be reduced to Rs.600. We therefore need to adjust the EBIT for taxes and make it a post tax EBIT number.

Step 3: Subtract Fixed Capital and Working Capital Investment

Step 3 is the standard procedure we use to calculate free cash flow to the firm. Here, we will subtract our working capital and fixed capital investments from the amount derived by performing step 1 and step 2. The complications that may arise while doing so have been discussed in earlier s.

These three steps can be summarized in the following formula:

FCFF = (EBIT *(1-tax rate)) + Depreciation – FC Investment – WC investment

Calculating Free Cash Flow to Firm: Method 4: EBIDTA

The fourth method of calculating free cash flows is closely related to the third method. Here too we are being provided with excerpts from the income statement. Instead of being provided with the EBIT number, we are provided with the EBIDTA number.

EBITDA stands for Earnings before interest, tax, depreciation and amortization. As we can see this appears even further up on the income statement as compared to the EBIT number.

Here even the depreciation has not been subtracted. Hence there is a slight change in the step 1 that we followed above.

Change in Step 1: Add Back Depreciation Tax Shield

Since the depreciation amount has not been deducted, there is no need to add it back. However, the depreciation amount does reduce the tax bill of the company. Hence, we need to add back the depreciation tax shield to find out the true free cash flow that will accrue to the firm.

Notice the difference. When we were given EBIT, we added back the entire depreciation amount. In this case we will only add back the tax shield provided by the depreciation.

For example, if the depreciation amount was Rs.200 and the prevailing tax rate is 40%, we will add back only Rs.80 i.e. (Rs.200*0.4) and not the entire Rs.200 as we did in the earlier case.

Apart from this, steps 2 and 3 need to be repeated exactly as they were in the above case.

This method can be summarized in the following formula:

FCFF = (EBITDA*tax rate) + (Depreciation*tax rate) – FC Inv - WC Inv

Thumb Rule:

The thumb rule in these cases is to adjust for any non cash changes above the income statement metric that you have been provided. All non cash changed below the metric must be ignored or only adjusted for taxation.

It is for this reason that we added back the entire depreciation amount in case of EBIT. (Depreciation appears above EBIT on the income statement) whereas we add only the depreciation tax shield in the case of EBIDTA (Depreciation appears after EBIDTA on the income statement)

Thus, we can derive free cash flow to the firm from a wide variety of metrics. We could use the cash flow statement, the income statement or even some selected information from the income statement.

Calculating Free Cash Flow to Equity

We studied the different methods to calculate the free cash flow to the firm (FCFF) in the previous. In this , we will learn about how to derive free cash flow to equity (FCFE). Here too there are multiple methods involved. However, since we already have a background in calculating cash flows, we need not go into that much detail here.

The calculation of free cash flow to equity is closely linked to the free cash flow to the firm calculation. There are slight differences which need to be highlighted in this . To understand these differences we need to understand the concept of net borrowing.

Firms could be borrowing money and paying off debt at the same time. This could be because they are refinancing the debt at a cheaper interest rate. Alternatively, a firm could simply be rolling over its debt to maintain a target debt amount.

Hence there are inflows and outflows that occur as a result of this simultaneously. The firm's cash position will therefore experience simultaneous inflows and outflows. We need to consider only the net effect of these flows. This can be calculated in the following manner.

Net Borrowing = Long and short term debt issues – Long and short term debt repayments

This formula is of utmost important while calculating free cash flow to equity (FCFE) and will be used in each of the three cases possible.

Let's have a look at the details:

Case # 1: Deriving Free Cash Flow to Equity (FCFE) From Cash Flow to Operations (CFO)

We understood that the difference between free cash flow to the firm and the cash flow from operations was simply the investment in fixed assets. We do not consider investment in fixed assets to be a part of the cash flow from operations. However, we do consider it while calculating free cash flow to the firm. Hence we arrived at the formula:

FCFF = CFO – FC Investments

In case of free cash flow to equity (FCFE) we need to add one additional step. We need to account for borrowings as well. Now, we are only concerned with the cash that will be available for equity shareholders. Hence if we borrow more, more cash becomes available. If we pay off some debt, we are left with less cash. Notice we are talking about repayment of debt principal. The interest payments have already been accounted for.

Therefore, we need to consider the net effect of the borrowing as well to arrive at free cash flow to equity. The formula for the same is:

FCFE = CFO – FC Inv + Net Borrowing

Case # 2: Deriving Free Cash Flow to Equity (FCFE) From Net Income

Once again, lets understand the free cash flow to equity (FCFE) formula in contrast to the free cash flow to firm

(FCFF) formula. The formula for deriving free cash flow to firm (FCFF) from net income was:

FCFF = Net Income + Non cash Expenses + **After Tax Interest** – FC inv – WC Inv

Now, with regards to the after tax interest expenses, we do not need to add them back. As far as the cash flow to equity shareholders is concerned, interest expenses are included in the outflow and hence do not need to be added back.

Also, once again we need to add back the net borrowing figure since it affects that cash that is available to the equity shareholders. The modified formula therefore is

FCFE = Net Income + Non cash Expenses + **Net Borrowing** – FC inv – WC Inv

Case # 3: Deriving Free Cash Flow to Equity (FCFE) From Free Cash Flow to the Firm

Lastly, we have the simplest case of calculating free cash flow to equity (FCFE) if we are given free cash flow to the firm (FCFF) as input. Remember that the difference between free cash flow to equity (FCFE) and free cash flow to firm (FCFF) is only the debt part. Hence, we need to make 2 adjustments.

- The first adjustment will account for the interest part i.e. it will subtract post tax interest expense from free cash flow to firm (FCFF)

- The second adjustment will account for the principal part i.e. it will add the net borrowing to the calculation

Thus, to derive free cash flow to equity (FCFE) from free cash flow to firm (FCFF), the formula is:

FCFE = FCFF − Interest Tax Shield + Net Borrowing

It is therefore possible to calculate free cash flow to equity from various types of inputs.

Calculating Free Cash Flows: The Case of Preferred Shares

In the previous we understood how to calculate free cash flows which accrue to the firm as a whole as well as to equity shareholders. However, while conducting this analysis we made an implicit assumption. We assumed that there are only two classes of funds available to the firm, this is equity and debt.

This assumption is good in the theoretical world. It helps us form a basic understanding of how free cash flows work. However, this is not how it works in real life. In real life, many hybrid modes of finance can possibly be used. One of the commonly used modes is preferred shares.

Just to refresh your memory, preferred shares behave partly like debt and partly like equity. They have a fixed rate of return. However, it is not mandatory for the company to pay this fixed dividend if there is no profit in the current year. In this , we will concentrate on how preferred shares affect the calculation of free cash flows.

Preferred Shares: Treated Like Debt:

As far as the cash flows are concerned preferred shares must be treated like debt. This is because they have a fixed rate of return and in most circumstances companies will end up paying the dividend that is fixed on them. The similarity to debt makes this assumption realistic.

Preferred Dividends Are Not Tax Deductible:

However, there is a subtle difference between the treatments of interest paid on debt and dividends paid on preferred shares. Interest paid on debt is tax deductible. However, legally preferred shares are considered to be a part of equity. It is for this reason that any compensation paid to the preferred shareholders is not considered as an expense for tax purposes.

In simple words, preferred shares are not tax deductible. This makes it necessary to make certain modifications while calculating the free cash flow due to equity as well as to the firm. Let's discuss these modifications:

Calculating Free Cash Flow to Firm (FCFF):

The procedure to calculate the free cash flow to the firm (FCFF) remains the same. The only difference lies in the following adjustments:

- **Add Back Preferred Dividends:** Along with interest, we will also add back preferred dividends while calculating the free cash flow available to the firm. However, we usually reduce the interest tax shield from the interest amount. In case of preferred dividends, there is no tax shield. Hence the entire amount paid as preferred dividend simply needs to be added back to the cash flows to derive the free cash flow of the firm.

- **Adjust The Weighted Average Cost of Capital (WACC):**Also, the rate at which we discount the free cash flows has to be modified when we include preferred debt. Earlier we used to calculate WACC using only two components i.e. debt and equity.

Now, since there are three different modes of financing with three different costs, obviously our WACC will be the weighted average of all the three modes!

Calculating Free Cash Flow to Equity (FCFE):

While calculating free cash flow to equity, we have to use adjustment number one mentioned above i.e. add back preferred dividends. However, we must not use adjustment number two. This is because free cash flow to equity is discounted at cost of equity. It is not discounted at WACC.

However, there is another adjustment that is specific to the calculation of free cash flow to equity. The same has been mentioned below:

- **Adjust Net Borrowing:** Just like we made adjustments for debt while calculating free cash flow to equity, similarly we need to make adjustments to preferred equity as well.

  All repayments need to be subtracted from the free cash flow to equity whereas any cash raised by new issue of preferred shares must be added to the cash flows. Once again, we need to consider the net change in the position of preferred equity if the firm is issuing more shares and repurchasing the old ones simultaneously.

To sum it up, preferred equity is a fairly common mode of financing used by companies. The adjustments that need to be made to the standard process of calculating free cash flows are very intuitive and minor. If a student is well versed with calculating free cash flows, the inclusion of preferred equity will not make much of a difference.

Changes in Financing Policy: Effect on Free Cash Flow

While valuing firms, free cash flow has to be calculated over a number of years. Hence, there is a good chance that the firm may change its financing policies during such a long period. It is for this reason that we need to consider what happens to the cash flows in the event financing policies were actually changed. Analysts usually consider the fact that the cost of operations of a firm will change over time. They do consider factors like inflation, increase in the cost of raw material, increase in wages and so on. However, as we have seen the effect of changes in financing policy are never considered. In this , we will do the same.

So, the objective is to figure out what are the possible changes in financing policy that can actually happen. Then the next step is to figure out how the cash flow changes in the event of each of these policy changes.

Possible Financing Policy Changes:

Here are the changes which firms usually make to their financing policy:

1. *Change in leverage*
2. *Increase in Dividends*
3. *Share Issues*
4. *Share buybacks/repurchases*

Effect on the Cash Flows:

Let's first consider the case of effect on leverage and how it affects both measures of free cash flow i.e. cash flow to the firm and cash flow to equity.

Since we have considered the cases of share repurchase and share buybacks separately, the change in leverage can be zeroed down to one single factor i.e. the change in debt.

In the event of paying off a debt or raising new debt, there will be no effect on the free cash flow to the firm. This is because free cash flow to the firm considers the cash that will accrue to the firm as a whole and not to equity and debt holders separately.

However, the free cash flow to equity shareholders is affected when debt is paid off or raised. When a firm uses additional cash to pay off debt now, it's free cash flow to equity is reduced in the current year. However, this reduction is offset by an increase in free cash flow to equity in the forthcoming years since the debt has been paid off and does not have to be serviced.

In the event of the firm raising more debt, the exact opposite happens. The free cash flow to equity increases in the current year and falls down in the subsequent years. Hence, if an analysts suspects that the firm is going to change its debt policy in the future, they must account for it while calculating free cash flow to equity.

The Case of Increase/Decrease in Dividends, Share Issues and Share Repurchases:

The cases listed above as case number 2, 3 and 4 have been combined in this point. The reason for doing this is that all these cases work on the same logic.

Increase or decreases in dividends, share issues and share repurchases have absolutely no effect on the free cash flow to the firm or on the free cash flow to equity! Both these measures of cash flows are calculated from EBIDTA or from cash flow from operations.

EBIDTA appears before any financing effects on the balance sheet and cash flow from operations are calculated from the net income number. In either case, how the financing is done will have no effect.

This fact is often used by examiners to confuse students. Usually there will be information that is relevant and then one of the above points will be mentioned. Please remember that case numbers 2,3 and 4 have no effect on the free cash flows. Hence, the only change that a firm can make to its financing policy that can affect the firm's free cash flows is issuing more debt!

Single Stage FCFF Model

We now have a fair understanding of what the concepts of free cash flow to the firm is. We also know how to calculate this metric under various circumstances. It is now time to use this metric to arrive at the final valuation for a given firm which is the objective of the whole exercise.

The FCFF metric can be used in various ways to derive the valuation for a firm. One of the most basic ways is called the single stage FCFF model. In this we will have a look at this model. It is very basic and is usually not used by analysts. However, it helps in forming a strong base on which the concepts related to slightly complicated models can be built. So let's begin.

Similarity with Gordon Growth Model:

The best way to introduce this model will be to highlight its similarities with the Gordon Growth model. FCFF valuation is almost analogous to the Gordon model except that it uses other components as inputs to the calculation. Like the Gordon model, the single stage FCFF model calculates the value of the firm in two parts. The first part is called the horizon period. This is the period for which the analyst explicitly forecasts the value of the firm by explicitly forecasting the growth rates. Obviously this can only be done for a short period of time let's say 5 to 7 years.

However, the firm has a perpetual life and its value can only be calculated by using a perpetuity. This is accomplished by using a terminal value. Once again, the assumptions of the

Gordon growth rate model are followed. The long term growth rate that the firm is expected to achieve is always less than the long term discount rate which is being used. Only if this assumption is used, can a finite value be reached.

Differences with Gordon Growth Model:

There are some differences between the single stage FCFF model and the Gordon growth model. These differences stem from the different inputs that are used by the models:

- the single stage FCFF model uses Free cash flow to the firm as an input whereas the Gordon growth model uses dividends as an input to calculate the value of the firm
- the single stage FCFF model uses Weighted average cost of capital (WACC) at which the value of the firm is discounted whereas the Gordon model uses return on equity as the input
- Lastly, the single stage FCFF model has to make adjustments to include the after tax cost of debt while calculating the weighted average cost of capital.

Assumptions:

There are certain assumptions implicit in this model. First is the assumptions that the cash flows of the firm will not change much over the years. They are explicitly forecasted for some years and then a constant growth pattern is assumed. This model is therefore only useful for very mature companies who have extremely stable cash flows. Since these companies are few and far off, the usage of the single stage FCFF model in the real world is very limited

Secondly, there is this assumption that the long term growth rate will be less than the long term discount rate. This is the problem with all valuation models since the value of a firm would be infinite is its long term growth rate is more than its long term cost of capital.

Formula:

Lastly, the formula for calculating the value of the firm using the single stage FCFF model is as follows:

Terminal Value of the Firm = FCFF (1) / WACC – g

Where

FCFF (1) is the cash flow that accrues to the firm in the first year post the horizon period

WACC is the weighted average cost of capital

G is the long term growth rate

WACC itself is calculated as follows:

WACC = (w (E) * r (E)) + (w (D) * r (D) *(1-tax rate))

Using Target Capital Structure:

The intention behind conducting this analysis is to ensure that the future valuation of the company is known. Also, we are using the cash flows which will accrue in the future to arrive at the valuation. Hence, it only makes sense that the discount rate being used also depicts the future.

In many cases, the present capital structure as well as the target capital structure for the future may be mentioned in the question paper. Students are expected to use the target capital structure for calculation of the WACC.

This may sound counter-intuitive as present capital structure is a fact and the future capital structure is only a target which may or may not be used by the firm. However, it would still be advisable that the future target structure is used since even the cash flows being discounted are only an assumption!

Variations in Cash Flow Models

We are now aware of how to use the basic single stage models for both free cash flow to the firm (FCFF) and free cash flow to equity (FCFE). It is now time to look into more advanced models which involve two or more stages for which cash flows will be predicted. Now, we need to understand that there is no finite number of models for calculating the value of the firm using these metrics. We could have an infinite number of models, if we just tweak the assumptions pertaining to free cash flow to the firm (FCFF) and free cash flow to equity (FCFE) a little bit.

Listing down all the models which are used will overwhelm any students. Instead we must look at what causes the variations in these models. We will do so in this .

How Many Stages to Assume?

The first question we need to answer is how many stages of cash flow projections we need to assume at arrive at a fair valuation.

Let's first define what a stage means and why it is important. A stage of cash flow is a group of years wherein the cash flow of the firm will behave in a similar manner. For instance, if a firm will experience a 7% growth in its free cash flows for the next 5 years, then for calculation ease we can combine these 5 years into 1 stage and use a single formula to derive a valuation for all these five years.

The common variations used are two stage, three stage and even spreadsheet modeling wherein every year is considered separately and the concept of stages does not apply at all.

How to Decide the Number of Stages?

The number of stages that are used by the analyst in valuation are connected to the characteristic of the firm being valued.

- In case the firm being valued is a relatively new firm, then there are expected to be a lot of fluctuations in the free cash flow that accrue to the firm. In the first few years, the firm may experience a negative cash flow. In the forthcoming years, the firm may experience positive cash flows growing at a high rate and then the growth rate may fall down before finally the free cash flows stabilize. In this case, a three stage model may be relevant

- In case of relatively mature firm, there may be no negative cash flows. The growth rate of the cash flows may be expected to change because of the business cycles. Hence, in this case a two stage growth model may be more relevant

- In some cases, analysts may have access to specific information which may allow them to model in detail the cash flows that the firm will receive over a period of years. In such cases, spreadsheet modeling will provide a much more accurate estimate.

Hence, based on the characteristics of the firm, the relevant model may be decided.

Which Metric to Use?

The next question which arises is that which metric of free cash flow should be used. Would free cash flow to the firm provide a more accurate forecast? Or would free cash flow to equity be more relevant? This is a fairly simple question to answer. If we are only considering the point of view of equity shareholders, then we must use free cash flow to equity. In other cases, free cash flow to the firm may be used. So every model will have two variations like two stage model using free cash flow to the firm and two stage model using free cash flow to equity.

How to Estimate Free Cash Flow?

The next question pertains to how to calculate the growth rates for the cash flow metric choses. When we were using dividends, we had no option but to make assumptions regarding what the growth rate of dividends will be.

When it comes to free cash flows, we have two options:

1. For instance, we could just simply make assumptions about the growth rates of these cash flows in the forthcoming years. For instance, we may assume that the free cash flow to the firm will grow at 7% for the next 5 years. This will obviously provide a very rough and inaccurate value of the firm.

2. Secondly, free cash flows are open to more analysis. We could calculate what the movements in the individual components of the cash flows would be and derive the cash flows as a result. For instance, we could use changes in net borrowing and working capital investment as input and derive free cash flow to equity as output. This model is more accurate. However, it also necessitates that the analyst must have access to information about how the company plans to change its cash flows in future periods. For a short period of time, let's say 5 years, this information is obtainable. Beyond that, it is pure speculation since not even the company would be in a position to make an accurate forecast for such a long time horizon.